Cover Your Assets:
Lawsuit Protection

Cover Your Assets: Lawsuit Protection

How to Safeguard Yourself,
Your Family, and Your Business
in the Litigation Jungle

Jay W. Mitton, M.B.A., J.D.
with Ginita Wall, CPA, CFP

Crown Trade Paperbacks
New York

Copyright © 1995 by Jay Mitton

Published by Crown Trade Paperbacks, 201 East 50th Street, New York, New York 10022. Member of the Crown Publishing Group.

Random House, Inc. New York, Toronto, London, Sydney, Auckland

CROWN TRADE PAPERBACKS and colophon are trademarks of Crown Publishers, Inc.

Manufactured in U.S.A.

Design by Linda Kocur

Library of Congress Cataloging-in-Publication Data

Mitton, Jay.
    Cover your assets : lawsuit protection : how to safeguard
yourself, your family, and your business in the litigation jungle /
Jay Mitton with Ginita Wall. — 1st paperback ed.
    Includes bibliographical references and index.
    1. Executions (Law)—United States—Popular works. 2. Adversary
system (Law)—United States—Popular works. 3. Estate planning—
United States. I. Wall, Ginita. II. Title.
KF9025.Z9M58 1995
347.73'77—dc20
[347.30777]   95-9670
                                                             CIP

ISBN 0-517-88518-2

BVG 01

Contents

Cover Your Assets:
Lawsuit Protection

Chapter 1

Confronting the Lawsuit Jungle

Lawsuits can come out of the blue. So it seemed to Paul Smith, a southern California farmer, who was tilling his fields when he was served with a summons by the sheriff. A few days earlier Paul was saddened when a hired hand on the neighboring farm had been electrocuted when he touched a poorly insulated cable that ran to an implements shed. Paul's sadness turned to shock when he was served with the widow's lawsuit charging him with gross negligence in the installation of the cable, and asking for $1.3 million. Until he received the legal papers, he had forgotten that eight years earlier he had helped his neighbor install that very electrical cable. Paul was punished for a neighborly deed years after the event.

Could this happen to you? Certainly. More than 90 million lawsuits are filed in the United States each year, so your chances of being sued are statistically quite high. Everyone should take steps to protect themselves from loss through lawsuits. If you are in a profession or avocation that is particularly susceptible to lawsuits, you are particularly vulnerable, and it is imperative that you take protective action immediately. In this book you will learn how to take preventative measures to insulate yourself, your family, and your assets from loss.

While you can't conduct your day-to-day life with thoughts of lawsuits constantly at the forefront, you must develop a mental habit of defensiveness. As you work around your home or yard, be aware of hazards you may be creating for an unsuspecting child or adult. As you run your business, be alert to the possible consequences of your actions and inactions. Lawsuits in America have reached epidemic numbers. You must protect yourself.

My Story

I hold four college degrees (A.S., B.S., M.B.A., and J.D.) and have taught as a university instructor. I am the senior partner of a California, Texas, and Utah law firm with a national practice in the highly specialized field of advanced estate planning and asset protection. My clients include movie stars, professional athletes, and many businesses, both large and small. I have lectured on the subject of lawsuit and asset protection at more state and national conventions and seminars than any lawyer in the United States. I have also trained more attorneys in this field than any other professional.

Lawsuit and asset protection has been my mission ever since childhood. As a young boy, I saw my father, a successful building contractor, lose everything. My father was a decent man and a good businessman, but he was caught in the lawsuit jungle.

One day a neighbor asked my father if he could borrow a newly acquired dump truck. While driving the truck, the neighbor lost control and crashed into someone's property, causing considerable damage. Because it was my father's truck, he was held liable. My father had no insurance for such losses, so he had to pay personally.

Another neighbor in Boise, Idaho, asked my father if he could charge a few things on my father's account at the local lumber store. He would pay Dad right back, he promised. After charging most of the construction materials for his new home, he filed for bankruptcy, once again leaving my father liable for considerable debts because he had done a favor for a neighbor.

About the same time, my father built a show home, furnishing the home on credit. The people who bought the home wanted the furniture as well, and agreed to pay the furniture store. Unfortunately, they did not, and my father, though innocent, was held responsible and had to pay for the wrongdoing of another.

My father lost everything, and I spent much of my childhood eating bread and milk for breakfast, lunch, and dinner. I decided that when I grew up, no one would ever take one penny from Jay Mitton in a lawsuit. I became an attorney, and I have dedicated my life to helping people avoid the financial catastrophes that beset my family.

Circumstances That Generate Lawsuits

Lawsuits fall generally into two broad categories: acts of omission, and acts of commission.

Acts of Omission

This type of liability occurs when you should have taken action but didn't, although the law imposes upon you the duty to act, speak, or intervene. Many malpractice suits against doctors arise from acts of omission. For example, a doctor examines a patient but fails to discover the slow-growing cancer, or a dentist doesn't comment on a small growth developing in a patient's mouth, which is later discovered to be malignant.

Acts of Commission

In acts of commission, liability arises from the intentional or negligent acts you commit when you should have known that such an act could harm or injure another. For example, a doctor performs surgery but is careless in the suturing. Or an employer lets an employee run errands in the employer's uninsured or defective automobile, and the employee is injured in an accident.

Actions That May Result in a Lawsuit

Whether the lawsuit is due to your act of omission or act of commission, the impact can be devastating to you emotionally and may ruin your financial health. Following are some typical situations in which you could be exposed to a lawsuit. We will be discussing them in more detail in later chapters.

> • One of your children causes an accident. For example, your child breaks a neighbor's window or sets fire to a neighbor's property. Frequently the courts will hold parents responsible for the negligent acts of their children, especially if the parent

could have taken preventative measures to preclude an injury, such as supervising the child properly, as discussed in Chapter 2, "Avoiding Liability
for the Acts of Your Children."

• You are an officer, director, or volunteer of a corporation or nonprofit organization that has a lawsuit
filed against it. Volunteers and paid employees are
held liable for their own wrongdoing, of course, but
officers and directors who engaged those volunteers and employees, or who failed to supervise
them or set up safeguards to prevent their malfea-
sance, can also be held liable, as you'll learn in Chapter 3, "The Dangers of Volunteer Work."

• You are an officer or director of a business that is
sued. Increasingly, officers and directors are personally sued for damages where the action of the
board on which they serve creates liability, or
where their negligence or misconduct causes
harm. This is covered in Chapter 4, "The Risks of
Serving as an Officer or Director."

• You gave advice, even free advice, that results in
injury to someone. Today, you can even be sued by
someone who relied on the advice you gave someone else if you could have foreseen that others
would rely on your advice. To learn how to avoid
this, read Chapter 5, "Avoiding Liability for Giving
Advice."

• Your name is used in an endorsement, or even on
a bank account. It can be very dangerous to allow
your name to be used in promotions of products or

investments, or even to let your name be placed on someone else's bank account, as you'll see in Chapter 6, "Avoiding the Pitfalls of Allowing Your Name to Be Used by Others."

• You guarantee an obligation of someone who doesn't pay. Read Chapter 7, "The Dangers of Guaranteeing Obligations."

• Someone is injured at your home, caused, for example, by a break in the pavement or a failure to maintain your walkway. You can be held liable for injury to a guest, whether invited or not. The courts generally hold that if a dangerous condition exists on your property that you know about or should have known about, you can be liable for resulting injuries. To protect yourself, see Chapter 11, "Protecting Your Home from Lawsuits."

• A defect is discovered in property you've sold. Hidden defects in any property you sell—be it real estate, used vehicles, or appliances—can result in a lawsuit if the purchaser wasn't aware of the defect, as discussed in Chapter 12, "Selling Property Without Being Sued."

• You are involved in an automobile or recreational vehicle accident that results in injury or property damage. Insurance is important, and you must read the fine print to make sure it covers your activities. To learn about this, see Chapter 16, "Choosing the Best Insurance for You."

• Your partner's negligence results in a suit against you. The risks are very high that if your business partner or associate does something wrong, a patient or customer will sue you for his negligent acts. To learn how to avoid this, see Chapter 19, "Limited Partnerships Will Protect Your Assets."

• You are accused of professional malpractice. For example, a doctor negligently recommends the wrong course of treatment and the patient dies. Adequate liability insurance is your best defense, but awards sometimes exceed the amount of insurance you carry, or exclusionary clauses can render your insurance worthless, as you'll learn in Chapter 23, "How to Protect Against Customer Lawsuits."

• An accident is caused by your employee for which you may be legally responsible. An employer may be held liable for employee negligence if an accident occurs while an employee was engaged in business activities. To protect yourself, read Chapter 24, "How to Protect Against Lawsuits Involving Employees."

How to Hold Assets

At the heart of lawsuit protection is the manner in which you hold title to assets and the way in which you structure your business affairs. I believe that incorrect planning in these areas causes more loss each year than most natural disasters, and unlike natural disaster, they can be avoided.

Joint ownership of assets is the most frequent form of asset ownership, but it can be particularly devastating, as you will learn in Chapter 8, "The Dangers of Joint Ownership."

Other elementary forms of asset protection include placing title in children's names, putting assets in the name of your spouse, and titling property as tenants in common or tenants by the entireties. These have their drawbacks, and more advanced asset protection devices will better protect your personal assets as you'll see in Chapter 9, "How to Take Title to Your Personal Assets."

Living trusts are very popular as a way to avoid probate, but they also offer some lawsuit protection. Even better protection is available with more advanced trusts, as discussed in Chapter 10, "How Living Trusts Can Protect Your Assets."

Most businesses should be incorporated for best lawsuit protection. But you must be careful in structuring your corporation, or it might give no protection at all. Read Chapter 17, "How to Establish Superior Business Lawsuit Protection," and Chapter 18, "The Advantages of Corporations for Businesses and Professionals."

Limited partnerships offer superior protection for many personal and business assets, especially family limited partnerships. They are covered in Chapter 19, "Limited Partnerships Will Protect Your Assets."

How to Use This Book

As you can see, you are not only vulnerable to a lawsuit for your own actions or inactions but you also may be held liable for the acts of others, such as an associate, partner, or employee. Review the list above, then turn to and read as many of the chapters that pertain to you. Many readers will find that *all* the chapters are relevant to them. Each chapter describes situations to avoid, how to stay alert to potential problems, and steps you should take now to protect yourself. This may involve correctly setting up your business or making major modifications to your existing business. It also often means restructuring the way in which you hold title to personal assets so as to provide yourself with the greatest lawsuit protection. The discussions in each chapter will direct you to the chapters on legal entities that protect assets; thus you can learn more about the specific techniques that will protect your assets in each situation.

Throughout the book I have provided case histories to illustrate particular problems. Where the facts are taken from a court case, I have indicated the case in a note, which you may look up at a law library if you want more information. Where the facts are from my client files, I have changed the names, cities, and a few of the inconsequential facts to protect their identities.

Action Checklist

❑ Develop mental defensiveness and stay alert to circumstances that could result in a lawsuit.

❑ Read the chapters that apply to your situation.

❑ As you read, make a list of things you should do to protect your assets from creditors or lawsuits.

Part I

How to Protect

Your Personal

Assets

Chapter 2

Avoiding Liability for the Acts of Your Children

Did you know that you can be held liable for the acts of your children, or even your grandchildren? That news came as a shock to the mother of two boys throwing snowballs on a winter day. One snowball broke a car's windshield, injuring the driver's face with bits of glass and gravel. The court held the mother liable for the "willful and malicious acts" of her sons.[1]

In New York, parents were held liable after their son stabbed a young girl in the back. The court held that it is a parent's duty to control his or her children's use of dangerous instruments and awarded a substantial judgment.[2]

A young Colorado boy and his friend were riding a snowmobile when the boy lost control. The passenger was severely injured, and sued the driver of the snowmobile and his mother. The insurance company refused to provide any coverage, since off-road vehicles are excluded from most vehicle policies unless the vehicle is licensed for use on public roads. The mother was held personally liable for damages caused by her son.[3]

Even grandparents must supervise their grandchildren. A Missouri couple were on the hook for $350,000 after their thirteen-year-old granddaughter crashed a jeep into a ravine, causing serious injuries to the girl. The court held that the grandparents had a duty to supervise the granddaughter and should not have allowed her to operate a potentially dangerous vehicle.[4]

Many states now have statutes that make parents responsible in varying degrees for damages caused by the willful, malicious, intentional, or unlawful acts of their children whether or not the parent knew of the minor's actions. Not all states have such statutes, but there is a clear and decisive trend toward increasing parents' liability for the acts of their children.

For example, in California, any act of willful misconduct can be attributed to the parent or guardian of the child, and the parent is liable for damages not exceeding $10,000 per act or injury. New York and Florida apply similar rules to minors who live with a parent, but the damages are limited to $2,500. And there are many circumstances when the amounts of recovery can far exceed the statutory amount. For example, parents can be held liable far in excess of the limits described above where the child is an employee of the parent, or is acting under the coercion or direction of the parent.

A juvenile who was hospitalized went on a rampage with his roommate in a Maryland hospital, extensively damaging his room and the surrounding area. The father was required to pay for the damages.[5]

In New York, however, the parents weren't liable when

their son threw a tennis ball down the stairs of a dark basement, injuring another child. Because the parents could not have anticipated such a remote accident, they weren't held liable for their son's negligent actions.[6]

Actions for Which Parents May Be Liable

Here are a few of the situations in which parents may be held liable for the acts of their children:

- if the child's acts have been habitual or the child has previously demonstrated inclinations toward such an act
- if parents have observed the child's destructive or vicious tendencies in the past
- if the parent has custody of the child but does not exercise effective control
- if the parents could reasonably foresee harm to another resulting from the child's predictable, irrational, or dangerous behavior
- if the parent allows a child to possess or use dangerous instruments such as a car, guns, knives, alcohol, or weapons
- if the child is employed by the parent
- if the parents consent, initiate, or ratify the acts of the child.

In addition to these acts, California law makes parents liable for negligent supervision that results in rape, murder, robbery, and so on. Wisconsin makes parents liable for teenage pregnancies, and parents can be fined up to $10,000 or two years in prison for failure to support grandchildren born of such pregnancies. Detroit makes parents liable for underage drinking by their children, and Arkansas holds the parents liable for a child's habitual absence from school.

A parent may even be *criminally* responsible for acts of his child if they were done at the parent's direction or with his consent. In one case a teenager served alcohol at a party in his home. After the party, a guest was injured in a car accident in which alcohol consumption was a factor. The court held that the parents of the party-giver were liable for their son's wrongdoing because they had given their consent for a party where they could have anticipated that alcohol would be served.[7]

Car owners are responsible for damages caused by family members, and in many states car owners can be liable for damages caused by others who drive their cars, as long as the owner consented to the use. In addition, most states hold the legal owner who allows an incompetent driver to use his car liable for any damage caused by the incompetent driver.

Actions for Which Parents Are Not Liable

Parents generally will not be held liable for the acts of their children in these situations:

- if there have been no past, prior, or habitual acts that would indicate that there is a problem with the child
- if the parent has not seen, and is not aware of, past vicious or criminal tendencies of the child
- if the child is not under the parents' direct or indirect control (even if the baby-sitter is with the child, the parent can still be held liable, as the parent is presumed to be in control of the baby-sitter, and therefore is in indirect control of the child)
- if the child was not supervised in a situation where normally a parent wouldn't have believed supervision was necessary.

The Trend—The Solution

As states expand laws that impose liability on parents for the acts of their children, the number of suits under those laws grows by leaps and bounds. Recently, an innocent victim of a gang's drive-by shooting filed suit against the gang members' parents for allowing their children to engage in gang activities. If you are a parent, talk to your insurance agent to be sure that civil liability for the negligent acts of your child will be covered under your homeowner's policy. The traditional fire and extended coverage policies generally do not provide such protection, but a broad-form homeowner's policy may provide substantial protection for the negligent acts of a child. Kids will be kids, but as laws increasingly hold parents responsible, you must insure yourself against potential liability.

Action Checklist

❑ Review your child's daily routines to be sure the child is properly supervised.

❑ Warn your child about the potential hazards of pranks, careless actions, and hazardous situations.

❑ Review your homeowner's and automobile insurance policies with your insurance agent to be sure any negligent acts of your children or other drivers will be covered.

Chapter 3

The Dangers of Volunteer Work

After a seminar I gave in the Midwest, a well-dressed woman approached me, anxious to share her story. She had served for a number of years on the board of a local community mental health group. One day the board voted to terminate the services of one of the paid employees, and a nightmare began for this woman who had given hundreds of hours, without pay, to this organization. The terminated employee filed a $3.2 million lawsuit against the board members. For more than three years the woman lived through meetings, hearings, and depositions that lasted as long as six hours. Describing her experience as "a living hell," she told me she would never again serve on the board of a charity.

Unfortunately, her situation is not unique, though her solution is drastic. While you must be increasingly on guard if you are involved in any kind of charitable or community service, there are ways that you can render charitable service and still protect your assets from lawsuits.

In the past, charitable institutions had legal immunity, but that is rarely true today. In general, charitable organizations are as liable as anyone else for their wrongdoing or negligence. Likewise, the officers and agents of a charity are required to act with diligence, care, and skill, and may be individually liable for injury if they fail to do so.

As plaintiffs and trial attorneys recognize that charities sometimes have brimming coffers and officers and directors with above-average net worth, we will see more and more charitable organizations finding themselves the target of lawsuits. The general trend is for the plaintiff to sue for any damage sustained in any way and to name, as a defendant, anyone even remotely connected to the damage. In addition, more and more charities are carrying insurance. Plaintiffs and their attorneys know that these insurance companies can afford to compensate for negligent actions that may have caused injuries, and so charities and their officers and directors find themselves increasingly vulnerable to lawsuits.

As a board member, you must remember that *you may be held liable for the act of a volunteer or employee of your charitable organization.* And a volunteer who is negligent may create liability for the charity's innocent officers and directors. In Virginia, a scoutmaster was criminally charged for sexual molestation of a child while the child was a Boy Scout. The parents also sued the local Boy Scout council of volunteers who had hired the sex offender. The court held the council negligent and liable to the child for physical and psychological harm.[1]

Sexual harassment suits are on the increase, as are other

suits for physical and mental harm caused by charity workers and clergy. Although the charitable organization itself may be unaware of the wrongdoing, the worker's or clergyman's activities can generate expensive lawsuits. And lawsuits can even be brought against the highest levels of the organization. For example, a recreational outing for members of a charitable organization ended in a tragic accident. When two members died, not only was the local organization sued but also its national and world headquarters. Thus there is now a trend toward decentralization of structure and use of multiple entities to protect charities from just this sort of predicament.

If you serve on a board, always request that you be named personally as an "insured person" under the charity's liability protection insurance policy. Simultaneously, have the charitable organization provide you with a written indemnification agreement that provides coverage and protection for you by the charity itself. This means that the charity promises to insulate you from any losses you might suffer while serving as its officer, director, or board member. In a recent case, the officers, directors, trustees, administrators, members, and shareholders of a charitable hospital that was sued were protected because the insurance policy listed them as "insured persons." This insurance policy covered the damages awarded to the injured person and protected the hospital board members from personal liability.

Action Checklist

If you decide to serve as an officer, director, or volunteer of a charity, I recommend the following action:

❑ Get a written indemnification agreement from the charity.

❑ Insist on being listed as an "insured person" on the charity's liability protection policy.

❑ Plan for the worst, and assume that you will at some point be the target of a lawsuit against the charity. Have in place the legal instruments and tools we discuss in Chapter 9, "How to Take Title to Your Personal Assets," including trusts, corporations, and partnerships that provide individual protection of assets.

Chapter 4

The Risks
of Serving as an
Officer or Director

When I speak at conventions about protecting your assets, I always discuss the liability you face when you serve in management of a company. During a break at a convention in Miami, a woman took me to task. "My father is here with me tonight, and after hearing you talk, he handed me a letter resigning as vice-president of my corporation," she complained.

Officers and Directors Can Be Sued

Throughout America, when a corporation gets sued, the officers and directors of the corporation are frequently personally sued as well. Officers and directors are personally liable for damages where their negligence or misconduct causes harm. A director may be held liable for an act of the board unless he specifically votes against a course of action.

For example, an attorney who is the director of a bank was in London on business when in his absence the other bank directors made a decision that resulted in a massive lawsuit against the bank. The bank was sued for millions of dollars, and its directors were named in the suit. The absent director was also held liable for the decision made in his absence, because he did not promptly object to the decision taken by the other directors in his absence.

You can be held liable even if you don't meaningfully participate in management. A Los Angeles physician who agreed to be listed as a director of his son-in-law's Seattle business was shocked when the Internal Revenue Service levied his medical practice bank account for $357,000 in delinquent payroll taxes owed by the Seattle corporation.

You could be liable if you serve on the board of a nonprofit organization (see Chapter 3 for more discussion). In a recent court case, officers of a religious organization were named in a $39 million lawsuit, and in another case a director was held personally liable for money owed to a plumbing company by the nonprofit corporation.

People embellish their résumés by serving on several boards of directors. But today you should think carefully before you agree to serve on any board.

Reasons for Which Officers and Directors Are Sued

Both corporate officers and directors owe specific and similar duties to corporations. Examples of such duties are:

- an undivided, unselfish, and unqualified loyalty
- scrupulous care never to profit personally at corporate expense, and

- unbending disavowal of any opportunity that would permit private interests to clash with those of the corporation.

Courts are widely expanding the traditional theories under which corporate officers and directors are held liable. The following is a partial list of reasons for which individual liability has been found in cases involving corporate officers and directors:

- improper guarantees by or on behalf of the corporation
- sale of controlling interest
- profiting from inside information
- short-swing profits
- failure to timely disclose material facts
- transactions with other companies in which officers or directors have an interest
- violations of specific provisions of articles or by-laws
- willful wrongdoing
- excess retained earnings
- failure to file annual report or to pay corporate taxes
- failure of corporate officers and directors to inspect corporate books and records
- failure to register corporation in other states
- inadequate investigation of facts included in public filings
- informal dissolution or liquidation of corporation
- loans to officers, directors, or stockholders
- patent, copyright, or trademark infringement
- acts beyond corporate powers
- aiding and abetting misconduct of others
- causing the corporation to incur unnecessary tax liabilities

- civil liabilities on account of registration statement prospectuses
- conflicts of interest
- corporate debts and delinquencies
- dishonored corporate checks
- excessive dividend payments
- extension of credit where not warranted.

Eleven Mistakes Your Corporation Must Not Make

A judge once told me that in almost every case that came before him where the issue of director and officer liability was raised, he allowed the action to proceed against both the corporation and the officers and directors. He said that he found there were eleven common major mistakes made by corporations and the individuals who run them that justified this imposition of personal liability:

- failure to have regular board of directors' meetings
- failure to have an annual shareholders' meeting
- failure to issue the corporate stock or maintain the stockholders' ledger
- failure to maintain up-to-date corporate records
- failure to have the required initial organizational meeting
- failure to adopt corporate by-laws
- failure to maintain proper accounting records
- failure to advertise and serve notice that the business was operating as a corporation
- failure to transfer assets into the corporation
- failure to get the proper state and local business licenses in the name of the corporation
- failure to file annual state and federal report forms.

This list is not all-inclusive, but it does give some general guidelines on those areas that are frequently overlooked, thus allowing the corporate liability shield to be pierced.

Shareholders Can Be Sued

In general, shareholders cannot be sued for acts of a corporation, but there are exceptions to that rule. Even if you are only a shareholder, if you participate in the decision-making of the corporation, you may be held to be an "implied officer." In a recent case, a creditor sued a roofing company for payment, and also named the company shareholder in its suit. The court held that the shareholder exerted effective control over the corporation because of his extensive involvement, and thus he could be held personally liable.[1] This is called "piercing the corporate veil." In cases where the courts allow the corporate veil to be pierced, the creditors are allowed to reach not only corporate assets but also the personal assets of the shareholder. A creditor may collect a corporate debt from a shareholder if the debt is personally guaranteed by the shareholder, if the corporation is completely bogus, or if the corporation is merely the alter ego of the shareholder.

Managers Can Be Sued

Increasingly, business managers and office managers themselves are liable individually for decisions and actions taken by them in the course of their employment. This has been particularly true of late in actions commenced by the Internal Revenue Service.

Under Internal Revenue Code Sec. 6672(a), any person required to collect and pay taxes can be held liable for the taxes plus a 100 percent penalty. That means any responsible person can be held liable, not just officers or directors. In a recent case a manager had authority to determine which creditors would be paid, and that was held to be sufficient for him to be liable for all the back taxes.[2]

In another case the IRS imposed a 100 percent negligence penalty on an office manager for failure to pay corporate withholding taxes, even though he did not have the authority to pay bills. Because this office manager had completed the forms necessary to maintain a line of credit for his employer, the IRS declared him a "responsible person" who could be held liable for the taxes of the business.

Three Things Corporate Directors or Officers Must Do

If you are presently serving as an officer or director, there are three things you should consider doing immediately.

1. Obtain an Indemnification Agreement and Insurance

I believe it is critical that you obtain from the corporation an indemnification that says you will be compensated for any suits that you may become involved in as a consequence of your service as an officer or director of the corporation. But remember, if the corporation is hit with a major lawsuit and ends up bankrupt, the indemnification agreement would be impotent because the corporation would have no funds with which to reimburse you. If possible, go beyond the indemnification agreement and request that the company purchase liability insurance to protect you. Many insurance companies offer policies that provide such protection to boards of directors and officers. Unfortunately, the cost of the insurance is rising rapidly, and can be a burden to many corporations.

2. *Act Prudently in Your Role as an Officer or Director*

As a director, you may be absolved from liability in the event of a lawsuit if you can demonstrate that you did not attend meetings where key decisions were made or, if you did attend and objected to certain decisions that later became the subject of a lawsuit, you had the secretary record your personal objection in the minutes of the meeting. In addition to promptly registering objections and having them recorded, always govern yourself by the "prudent man rule," which is to focus on the basic, direct attributes of common sense, practical wisdom, and informed judgment. To comply with the prudent man rule, directors need to establish a record of diligence and care. Govern all of your actions by this standard, which is applied in almost all liability situations.

3. *Insulate Your Personal Assets*

As an officer or director you might still be sued despite all your precautions. You can, however, insulate your personal assets by putting into trusts and partnerships the title to your home, your real estate, your bank accounts, stocks, bonds, mutual funds, and other investments. You will become acquainted with many of these methods in coming chapters (see Chapter 9, "How to Take Title to Your Personal Assets," Chapter 10, "How Living Trusts Can Protect Your Assets," and Chapter 19, "Limited Partnerships Will Protect Your Assets"). Most people should consider setting up family limited partnerships, which afford excellent insulation from lawsuits (if set up correctly), placing assets into the living trust of the less vulnerable spouse, and/or putting assets into certain irrevocable trusts.

Action Checklist

❑ Don't serve on the board of directors or as an officer of any corporation in which you are not directly involved.

❑ Obtain an indemnification agreement from any employer for whom you are a manager or have any position of authority.

❑ Obtain an indemnification agreement and directors' liability insurance from any corporation for whom you serve as an officer or director.

❑ Act prudently when dealing with or on behalf of a corporation (see list of reasons for which individual liability has been found in cases involving corporate officers and directors, pages 24–25).

❑ If you object to action taken by the board of directors on which you serve, promptly make your objections known and have the secretary record them in the minutes.

❑ Insulate your personal assets by creating trusts and partnerships to hold title, thus protecting yourself in the event of lawsuits.

Chapter 5

Avoiding Liability
for Giving Advice

Giving advice can be grounds for a lawsuit, even if it is gratuitous advice for which you are not paid. A real estate agent showed a home to a friend who liked it very much. The agent later mistakenly thought that the home was being sold at a public foreclosure auction, and induced his friend to bid on it. When the friend was the highest bidder and found out that he had paid $150,000 for a completely different home, he sued the agent and his broker for negligent advice, and both were found liable.[1]

An ill man called a doctor and received the wrong advice; the sick man subsequently died. The court held the doctor liable for his negligent telephone advice.[2]

In the past, you could be sued only by someone to whom you directly communicated your advice, but today a professional may be held liable for malpractice even by someone to whom he *never* gave advice. For example, an accountant was hired by a husband to prepare joint tax returns, but he failed to tell the wife that as a joint filer with her husband, she could be held liable for all the income taxes if her husband did not pay them. When the husband defaulted in his tax obligation and the wife was required to pay, the courts held that she could sue the accountant for negligence even though he had been hired by her husband.[3]

It is difficult to predict how the courts will treat such a third-party claim for negligent advice. In another case, an accountant told his client about an investment that later turned out to be a sham. When the investment went bankrupt, the accountant was sued by another couple whom the original client had told of the investment. An Alaska court held the accountant not liable, since he could not have reasonably foreseen that the information would be passed on to third parties.[4] In a similar case in New Jersey, an accountant was held liable whether or not he intended other parties to receive the information.[5] Most courts have adopted the "foreseeable test" for liability, which means that you can be held liable to anyone whom you could reasonably have foreseen would have relied on your advice.

An individual made a bad investment on recommendation of his broker, who told him that the investment would provide good cash flow without risk. The investor suffered substantial monetary losses, and the court found that the investment was inappropriate for the investor's income level. Both the broker and the broker's employer were liable for the investor's damage.[6]

In a similar case, an investment adviser had put all the risks of the investment in writing, and the investor acknowledged receiving the document. The court held that the adviser did not need to tell the client orally of the risks, and could reasonably assume that the investor would read the written documents outlining the risks. The adviser was not held liable for damages.[7]

The Reliance Factor

In order for someone to claim your advice caused them damage, they must have justifiably relied upon it. Many advisers have successfully defended their advice by carefully phrasing their recommendations. For example, a professional might say to a client, "I don't have all the facts on this investment, but based on what I know it is my personal opinion that you might consider it after you have personally weighed the risks involved." The courts have frequently held that one may be guilty of fraud if he states as a fact that which is only opinion.

Even Innocent Associates
May Be Sued for Advice Given by Another

Generally *if an employee gives false or negligent advice, not only is the employee liable but the employer, partners, and other associates may also be held liable.* An attorney giving negligent advice will find that the law firm itself may be held liable as well. An accountant can be sued and a judgment also rendered against his or her accounting firm. A stockbroker who gives advice can make the company with which he is associated fully accountable. This is why companies now often restrict employees from giving advice on certain subjects, having them sign employment agreements and providing specific training for employees as to the scope of their ability to give advice.

An employer may be absolved of liability where the employee did not give advice in his employment capacity. For example, an attorney and an acquaintance invested in an unsuccessful apartment complex venture; the acquaintance subsequently sued both the attorney and his law firm, claiming he had relied on the attorney's negligent advice. The court concluded that no attorney-client relationship existed, and that giving investment advice was outside the scope of the employee's duties. These were just two people who had made a bad investment and one of them happened to be an attorney.[8]

The Dangers of Giving Advice on a Subject for Which You Are Not Trained, Qualified, or Licensed

You run a significant risk of lawsuits if you give advice on matters for which you are not trained or properly prepared. For example, an employee of an investment company recommended a limited partnership interest as an excellent investment that would provide considerable shelter from income taxes. In fact, the limited partnership investment was completely wrong for the investor's financial situation and provided no tax shelter at all. The employee had little experience in evaluating limited partnership investments, and no formal training in the complex income tax rules concerning tax deductions from these types of investments. When the investment failed, the investor sued the employee and the investment company and won, claiming he relied on the employee's expertise in making his investment.[9]

In another case, investors interested in purchasing some property that was part of a bankruptcy proceeding relied on the tax opinion of an attorney, who was not a tax or securities expert. When the investors suffered losses and sued, the court found that the attorney's advice was negligent, "given with reckless disregard for its truth or falsity."[10]

Action Checklist

❑ Think carefully before you give someone advice. Don't give advice for which you do not have all the facts.

❑ Carefully phrase your oral recommendations so that the listener knows it is your personal opinion, and subject to his or her verification.

❑ Follow up an oral recommendation with a written memorandum, so there will be no misunderstandings.

❑ Carry malpractice insurance to cover you against giving negligent advice in your professional capacity.

❑ Never give advice on a subject for which you are not trained, qualified, or licensed.

Chapter 6

Avoiding the Pitfalls of Allowing Your Name to Be Used by Others

Your good name is a very valuable asset. Lending your name to another's venture can make your entire estate vulnerable to loss. Here's an example of what could happen.

A few years ago I advised a very prominent East Coast political leader in connection with some routine estate planning. He owned a .3 percent interest—three-tenths of one percent—in a land development project in California that had been given to him by a friend, and about which he knew very little. He had accepted the gift not realizing that his developer friend could now use the politician's name as a member of the real estate development team, inducing others to invest in their project. Furthermore, my client could now be held liable if anything went wrong and the other investors in the partnership later wanted their money back, or if the project was sued or went into bankruptcy. As general partners, each of the partners, including this man with a minimal interest, were fully liable for the acts of the other partners and activities of the partnership. We initiated action immediately to extricate him from this potentially lethal "gift."

Dangers of Letting Your Name Appear
on Someone Else's Business Bank Account

Many people have allowed their name to be placed on the bank account of a spouse, child, friend, relative, or employer, ignorant of the profound consequences. For example, a doctor adds his wife's name to the signature card for his business checking account so she can sign checks. Or a parent adds the children's names to an account, to avoid probate when the parent dies and to allow the children to get access to the funds in an emergency.

A Miami woman told me this story: "I let a friend put my name on his business account as a convenience, so I could sign checks for him if he were out of town or on vacation. His business was sued and went into bankruptcy. The court brought me in as a defendant and said that since I had allowed my name to be on the checking account I had rendered service as a constructive officer of the business. I was held liable for some of the debts and there is now a judgment against me for more than $2 million. I've lost my entire estate." The same thing happened in a Michigan court case, where a wife was held liable for back payroll taxes of a business owned and run by her husband.

Dangers of Allowing Your Name to
Be Used in Testimonials or Promotions

Two famous personalities have found that allowing their
names to be used in promotion of consumer products can create potential liability in consumer lawsuits and fraud investigations, as well as substantial adverse publicity. I am sure
these personalities did not anticipate the dangers involved in
granting permission for their names to be used in product en-
dorsements. Generally, you can be held liable if you allow
your name to be used in connection with false information,
that results in harm to another, if you did not exercise care in
ascertaining the accuracy of the information or in the manner in which that information was communicated. For example, if you are a prominent Idaho farmer who allows his name
to be used in a catalog advertisement for potato seed, and that
seed is later found to be diseased, you could be held liable.[1]
A similar outcome resulted where a celebrity endorsed a line
of shoes with defective slippery soles.[2]

Dangers of Serving as an Officer or
Director in Your Homeowner's Association

It has come as a shock to many that a business title or a minimal relationship with a company can bring massive liability.
Even an act as simple as serving as an officer in a homeowner's association can bring liability you may never have anticipated.

In a California case, a woman was molested, raped, and
robbed in her condominium late one night. The woman sued
the condominium association and the individual board mem-

bers for negligence, and won her suit.[3] Generally, a condominium association can be sued for negligent maintenance of the common areas by a member of the association, or by a member of the general public.

The Big Danger of a Little Involvement

A general partnership or a joint venture can bring awesome liability exposure to an unsuspecting partner. In an Alabama case, three new partners were added to a partnership about a year after the partnership had been formed. The new partners weren't told that the partnership had obtained a loan for $300,000 and that the funds had been spent by the previous partners. When the partnership business failed, only one partner was solvent. Though he owned only 6 percent of the partnership, the bank sued him for the entire $300,000 loan, of which he had previously been ignorant. Nonetheless, the court held that this new partner was liable for the full amount owed by the partnership. The $300,000 liability he had to pay back far exceeded his small interest in the partnership.[4]

The moral of the story is: If you are going to be a little involved in a big deal, then structure the deal as a limited partnership, a limited liability company or corporation, or some entity whereby liability can be regulated and you can be insulated from personal liability.

The Pitfalls of a Failed Limited Partnership

Although limited partnerships are less dangerous than general partnerships, they are not without pitfalls. A friend of mine found this out the hard way when the Internal Revenue Service sent him a bill for $265,000 in taxes because of an investment in a limited partnership that had entered bankruptcy. My friend had enjoyed accelerated tax benefits on paper losses during the early years of the partnership, and did not realize that when the partnership went bankrupt, a day of tax reckoning had come, and he owed substantial taxes on income that existed only on paper, called "phantom" income.

A limited partnership is supposed to limit the liability of limited investors, but this isn't always the case. I will never forget the retired woman who approached me at an Oakland convention where I was speaking to ask me why she had been named party to a lawsuit against the limited partnership. "I only invested $1,000, and they want me to pay $750,000," she said. "I thought that as a limited partner in a limited partnership, I couldn't be sued."

In theory, she was right, but very precise statutory steps must be complied with in the creation and execution of the partnership agreement. In this woman's case, the failure of the general partner to properly record the certificate of limited partnership resulted in the disqualification of the limited partnership. Since the limited partnership hadn't jumped through the required regulatory hoops, it was now considered to be a general partnership, and now all members, even those who thought they were limited partners, could be sued.

In a recent case in Illinois a purchase agreement was entered into before the requirements of a limited partnership were met. Eventually, the certificate for the limited partnership was filed, but it was filed in the wrong office. Because of the failed attempt to become a limited partnership, the defendant, who thought he was a limited partner, could now personally be held liable as a general partner.[5]

A limited partner must also take care not to act like a general partner by actively participating in the control and management of the partnership. In one case, the court held that the limited partners had not acted in their limited capacity but rather had exercised control over the limited partnership, and therefore could be held liable for the debt of the partnership.[6]

The Dangers of Selling a Business but
Allowing the Purchaser to Continue Using Your Name

The reputation of a successful small-business owner is of great value to a successor owner, who often wants to continue to use the previous owner's name to promote the business. This is fraught with danger. The public, upon seeing your name associated with the business, will presume that you are still involved in the business. If something goes wrong, years from now you may find yourself a surprised defendant in a lawsuit against a business you no longer own. When you sell a business, insist that the new owner use his name or the business name in promotional material, but not your name. Otherwise, plaintiffs may assert that you are maintaining a continued relationship as a general partner or joint venturer.

Even professionals have to be very cautious about consenting to the use of their names in promotional materials. In a recent case, a state supreme court entered an order of public reprimand against a prominent estate planning attorney who had consented to the use of his name in promotional materials prepared and distributed by others.

Remember, your name is a priceless asset that belongs to you alone. Avoid future grief and complications by vigilantly restricting the use of your name by others.

Action Checklist

❑ Do not let your name be used by others to promote investments in which you have an interest.

❑ Do not let your name appear on another person's bank account.

❑ Do not let your name be used in testimonials or promotions unless you have control over the content and context of such promotional materials, and can vouch for their accuracy.

❑ Do not serve as an officer or director of your home-owner's association unless it provides indemnification and director's liability insurance.

❑ Structure investment partnerships as limited partnerships rather than general partnerships, with your investment being a limited partnership interest.

❑ As a limited partner, avoid personal liability by not participating in management of the partnership.

❑ If you sell a business, do not allow the purchaser to continue using your name, or to imply that you are still in any way associated with the business.

Chapter 7

The Dangers
of Guaranteeing Obligations

A neighbor of mine was shocked to arrive home and see a notice taped to a telephone pole in front of his house proclaiming "This home will be sold at public auction to satisfy obligations." How had this happened? Three years earlier he had cosigned a bank loan for his son-in-law who was setting up a new optometry business. The business failed, and the bank foreclosed on my neighbor's home. Even though my neighbor had seen a couple of bank notices, his son-in-law had said, "Don't worry about a thing; I'm taking care of it."

This could happen to you. I know, because it has happened to me. I have guaranteed loans for two friends who reneged, and in both cases I had to pay off their loans. This was a chance I took, knowing the loans were not for substantial amounts, and I was prepared to pay if they did not.

When Should I Guarantee or Be a Cosigner?

When you sign a loan for someone else, the risks are high that the primary obligor will default, particularly if it is a new business being undertaken. *Whenever you sign a loan for someone else, you must be prepared to pay the obligation yourself.* If you are not, do not sign the loan. Unfortunately, when the primary obligor cannot pay, it forces an undue financial burden on the guarantor, and often results in the termination of the friendship or bad feelings that sometimes exist for years among family members who feel they have been wronged by the defaulting family member or friend.

There are many cases on this subject. For example, a cosigner on a $70,000 bank loan tried to wiggle out of liability, but the court held that he was just as liable for the loan as was the primary obligor.[1]

A mother cosigned on a car loan for her daughter. When the daughter defaulted, the mother claimed that the salesman told her that he only needed her signature as a formality and that she would not be financially obligated if she signed the papers. The court ruled that she should not have relied on the oral misrepresentation made by the salesman, and she was liable.[2]

Even loans cosigned for a spouse can be troublesome. A husband cosigned for his wife's student loan. They later divorced, and when the ex-wife defaulted her former husband was held liable. He declared bankruptcy, but was surprised to find that his obligation as a cosigner for his ex-wife's student loan wasn't released in bankruptcy under the laws of his state, and so he remained obligated to repay the loan.[3]

Limiting Your Exposure

The best way to limit your exposure is never to guarantee or cosign the obligation of another unless you have the means to be repaid if the obligor defaults (for example, you cosign for an employee, and you can withhold the amount due from his wages). If you are going to guarantee or cosign the obligation of another, it is extremely important to limit the scope of the guarantee. I always recommend to my clients that they limit the liability to a set time frame, such as one or two years, and a maximum amount. Unless you make specific limitations, you may unwittingly be assuming liability for all the obligations of the debtor.

One woman fell into this trap. She signed an agreement with the bank that stated, in part, "This guarantee is limited to an amount of $_____. If blank, this guarantee assumes payment of all obligations of the debtor plus interest and expenses of enforcing this guarantee. This guarantee shall apply to all obligations of the debtor made before, concurrently or after, to the extent of the liability indicated." The agreement she signed left the amount blank. She had obligated herself to pay the debtors' loans at any time he defaulted and in any amount, even if he borrowed the money years before she signed the agreement, or long after she had forgotten ever signing as a guarantor. Her liability was infinite. She could have limited her obligation by filling in the blank line, but she failed to do so. Consequently, she was held liable for the entire defaulted amount by the debtor.[4]

Guarantor vs. Co-maker

There is a legal distinction between a guarantor and a co-maker. A co-maker assumes a greater liability than does a guarantor, because the co-maker can be held liable whether or not the primary debtor becomes insolvent. A guarantor generally has secondary liability and becomes liable on the note only after the primary debtor defaults or becomes insolvent. (In some states, however, there is no distinction between the two categories; the guarantor is held jointly and severally liable with the primary debtor.)

Avoid guaranteeing or co-making loans whenever you can. If you feel forced because of family, personal, or business pressures to enter into an agreement, then consider being only a guarantor and not a co-maker. Above all, consider limiting the maximum amount of your exposure and the duration. For example, if you are guaranteeing an obligation, state in writing that the maximum amount for which you are at risk is $20,000 and the maximum term is two years from the date you sign the guarantee agreement, and that the guarantee cannot be extended beyond two years without a new document of guarantee signed by you.

Action Checklist

❑ Sign as a guarantor or co-maker of a loan only if you are prepared to pay the obligation yourself.

❑ Make sure you have a means of being repaid by the primary obligor if he or she defaults and you must pay the loan yourself.

❑ If you cosign, limit the liability to a set time frame, such as one or two years, and a maximum amount.

❑ If you must cosign on a loan, do so as a guarantor rather than as a co-maker.

Chapter 8

The Dangers of Joint Ownership

Joint Tenancy = Bad Estate Planning

In all my years as a practicing attorney, I have observed more estate planning disasters regarding joint ownership than in any other area of the law. Here are some examples.

A mother placed her entire $500,000 estate in joint ownership with her daughter. What Mom didn't realize is that when she dies, her daughter will receive everything and her son nothing, despite provisions to the contrary in her will. And if her daughter is sued or faces financial difficulties, all the money could be lost to the daughter's creditors.

A widow places her home in joint tenancy with her only son to avoid probate when she dies. But long before that, a customer of the son's automobile repair shop wins a judgment against him, and her home is seized to satisfy the debt.

An angry wife, whose name has been placed on her husband's accounts, withdraws all the money to run off with another man.

Another woman, recently married, dies just weeks after transferring all of her assets into joint tenancy with her new husband. Her three adult children inherit nothing.

Cases like these happen every day, and as unfair as the outcomes seem, they are upheld in court. In a Supreme Court case, parents had put their son's name on a bank account so it would automatically go to him when they died. But the IRS stepped in long before that, and seized the account to satisfy back taxes owed by the son.

When a person dies, property held in joint tenancy usually goes to the surviving joint tenants, rather than to the heirs named in the person's will. And if several of the joint tenants die, the remaining ones will own the property. For example, a husband and wife, shortly before their deaths, added their five children's names to the deed to their farm, creating a joint tenancy among the husband and wife and the children. The husband and wife died, and not long after that three of the children died. The farm now belongs to the surviving two children with no provision made for the heirs of the three deceased children. They are disinherited, though their grandparents' will shows that they intended to leave a portion of the property to them. Generally, a will has no legal effect over property held in joint tenancy. If the surviving children give some of their estate to their nieces and nephews, they could be socked with substantial gift taxes.

A few years ago, a widow in advanced stages of cancer asked me to review her will. I was shocked to find that although her will left her estate to her three children, she had placed her next-door neighbor's name in joint ownership with herself on her home and bank accounts, so he could assist her in paying bills. Had she died before seeing me, the entire estate would have gone to her neighbor, and her children would have received nothing.

There are times when joint ownership is appropriate. For example, joint ownership can be the most effective way to handle modest amounts of cash. My own daughter has a joint checking account with her mother that she uses to pay her incidentals and schooling expenses. And an adult child may have a joint account with an aging parent so he can assist in bill-paying.

Summary

Joint tenancy is the most frequent form of ownership of stocks, bonds, real estate, and bank accounts in the United States. Many financial advisers recommend joint tenancy because it avoids probate. But most people don't realize the dangers that exist if you own assets jointly with a spouse, parents, children, or a friend.

Improper use of joint ownership can:

- make the jointly held assets vulnerable to suits and judgments against any one of the joint owners
- make it easy for one of the joint owners to take all the jointly held assets without permission of the other joint owners
- supersede a will and make the will legally ineffective
- increase estate taxes at the death of the surviving joint owner.

Action Checklist

❑ Review all the assets you hold in joint tenancy.

❑ Consider changing joint tenancy to another form of ownership, such as individual ownership, trust, or limited partnership. See Chapter 9, "How to Take Title to Your Personal Assets," Chapter 10, "How Living Trusts Can Protect Your Assets," and Chapter 19, "Limited Partnerships Will Protect Your Assets."

Chapter 9

How to Take Title to Your Personal Assets

What's yours is yours forever, right? Wrong, say your creditors. Wrong, says the Internal Revenue Service. Wrong, says the bankruptcy court. People lose personal assets every day because of poor planning. Designing a plan to protect one's personal assets should be near the top of every American's list of objectives.

Imagine the grief of one woman who lost her home and its furnishings to the Internal Revenue Service after they disallowed deductions she had claimed from a failed tax-shelter investment. Twenty-seven bidders gathered for the auction in her home. She stood, tears streaming down her face, watching helplessly as her bedroom set was sold, then the dining room table, then the sofa. She sobbed as her television set was sold for $35 and hauled off by the successful bidder.

Many people try to protect their assets through elementary techniques such as joint ownership, placing title in the names of children or others, putting assets in the name of a spouse, or titling property as tenants in common or tenants by the entirety.

Joint Ownership

As we have already seen, joint ownership can be lethal, whether done for convenience or as asset protection. Creditors of the joint owner, including the IRS, can attach those accounts, as can the owner's disgruntled spouse in a divorce proceeding.

Placing Title in Children's Names

This can frequently protect assets from your creditors, unless the transfer is deemed fraudulent. A building contractor couple who had placed their home as well as their stocks, bonds, investments, and major bank accounts into the names of their children found that the creditors were unable to reach the $1.4 million of assets owned by the children when a lawsuit resulted in a judgment against the husband and wife. The court held that because the assets had been conveyed to the children sufficiently in advance of an anticipated lawsuit, the transfer did not violate the state's fraudulent conveyance laws. But keep in mind that placing assets in someone else's name gives that person complete control over the property, and you could end up losing everything.

Putting Assets in the Name of a Spouse

Sometimes this technique works. At a seminar, a building contractor told me that he had put everything in his wife's name. When he was later sued for $3 million, the assets in his wife's name were insulated from the judgment creditor. This man was lucky, because courts carefully scrutinize conveyances between relatives. Across the nation, it is widely recognized by the courts that husbands and wives, as well as other relatives, have exceptional opportunities to commit fraud on creditors. In fact, the very relationship between husband and wife has been found to be sufficient to show fraud and invalidate the transfer of property.

Titling Property as Tenants in Common

Tenants in common means that each owns an undivided interest in the property. Let's say that a husband, wife, and their son own a piece of real estate as tenants in common, each owning an undivided one-third interest in the property. In the event of a lawsuit against the son, his one-third interest can be seized or attached, but the two-thirds interest owned by his parents cannot. Therefore, this type of ownership can protect some family members, but it doesn't completely protect the assets.

Titling as Tenants by the Entireties

Twenty-four states recognize this form of joint ownership between husband and wife. Historically, property owned in this manner was protected from claims of creditors of one of the spouses, since each spouse is deemed to own the entire asset. But the protection of this form of ownership disappears if both spouses are sued.

Advanced Asset Protection Strategies and Entities

As you have now learned, the elementary strategies are often inadequate for asset protection in today's litigious society.

Accordingly, five legal entities are used increasingly by asset protection attorneys: revocable trusts, irrevocable trusts, limited partnerships, corporations, and limited liability companies.

Revocable Trusts

The public discovered revocable trusts through the best-selling 1950s book *How to Avoid Probate.* Today, the revocable trust is widely accepted; it is also known as a "living trust" and by some as a "loving trust." Once a revocable trust is created, the owner transfers assets to the trust. This is a very popular probate avoidance tool, because assets held in a living trust do not go through probate at death.

Many people are finding that there is some good, but not perfect, lawsuit protection available by using two revocable trusts, one for each spouse. Let's say that the husband is a doctor, vulnerable to malpractice lawsuits. If he conveys his assets to his wife's revocable trust, those assets will not generally be reachable by his creditors unless the transfer is found to be fraudulent. The longer the assets are held in the name of the wife's trust, the greater the degree of protection from a claim by the husband's creditors. The assets are vulnerable to attachment and seizure, however, if the wife is sued. A revocable trust cannot protect the assets of the trust owner from the trust owner's creditors.

Irrevocable Trusts

Irrevocable trusts are more complex than revocable trusts and are not used as frequently. An irrevocable trust is one that cannot be changed—that is, once you transfer assets to the trust, they remain the property of the trust until they are distributed to the trust beneficiaries under the terms of the trust. An irrevocable trust is generally effective for lawsuit protection only if the trustee, who manages the trust, and the beneficiary, who receives income and/or principal distributions, are individuals other than the person who set up the trust. If, for example, Dr. Smith puts assets into an irrevocable trust, names himself as the trustee, and provides in the trust agreement that the assets be used for his support, his creditors will generally be able to seize the assets. If, on the other hand, he names the bank as the trustee, and his children are the beneficiaries, he will have substantial lawsuit protection.

A word of warning: To be effective, your irrevocable trust must include two important legal provisions, the antialienation clause, and the spendthrift clause. Including these two clauses will add immeasurably to the protection capabilities of your irrevocable trust. The antialienation clause restricts the trustee from transferring trust assets to anyone other than the beneficiary, so a creditor of a trust beneficiary cannot receive any trust income or principal should the beneficiary renege on a debt. The spendthrift clause allows the trustee to withhold income and principal from a beneficiary if the trustee feels the money could or would be wasted.

A major disadvantage of the irrevocable trust is your loss of control over the assets, because someone else is now the trustee and manages the assets.

Limited Partnerships

The limited partnership is frequently one of the best ways to hold title to family assets for asset protection. This is because of a technical provision of the Uniform Limited Partnership

Act. Called the "charging order," it generally precludes an individual judgment creditor from seizing assets held by the partnership. I frequently advise my clients to place their personal and family assets—such as their homes, bank accounts, investments, and mutual funds—into one or more limited partnerships.

A limited partnership is a partnership having one or more general partners and one or more limited partners. The limited partners have limited liability for partnership debts, and limited control over the assets. The general partner may have only a small interest in the partnership, the rest owned by children or others, and yet still have full control over all of the assets of the limited partnership.

Corporations and Limited Liability Companies

These two forms of ownership are very popular, particularly for the operation of a business. (See Chapter 17, "How to Establish Superior Business Lawsuit Protection" for further discussion of these two types of companies.) Corporations are not often used for ownership of personal assets such as we have been discussing. Both the limited liability company and the corporation can be of great benefit in protecting business owners, managers, directors, and even business assets from litigation when designed correctly.

How to Handle Dangerous Personal Assets

Some assets are more dangerous than others from a liability standpoint. For example, I have a client who loves to fly, frequently taking passengers on a jaunt, and he allows his plane to be used by others. Another client has a large pleasure boat on which he entertains friends and business associates and their families, and he also lends his boat to friends and associates for their personal use.

Both of these clients own particularly dangerous personal items. They are vulnerable to lawsuits if anyone is injured, and the obvious initial solution to the problem is to carry plenty of liability insurance. But this may not be enough protection in the event of an accident; indeed, the typical personal liability policy may not cover an accident because of the business exception rules included within the policy. The owner may find himself completely liable and lose everything he owns.

Because insurance may not provide adequate protection, I frequently recommend the following approaches for dangerous assets:

- Convey the asset to a corporation, so that the corporation rather than the individual owns the asset.
- Transfer title to a limited partnership with its own unique set of liability protection laws.
- Have a limited liability company hold title to the assets.

A majority of states now recognize limited liability companies, which can be an effective means of protection because, by definition, generally only the entity itself is liable for any harm caused by the asset.

Each of these three approaches has advantages and disadvantages from an income tax standpoint and an estate planning standpoint. In my law firm, to solve dangerous asset problems we use a corporation or limited liability company about half of the time, and a limited partnership for most of the other cases. About 10 percent of the time, we use other miscellaneous tools and approaches. For example, for one client I transferred title of his airplane to a Nevada corporation. (In Chapter 20, "Which States Give the Best Lawsuit Protection," you will learn how the laws of Nevada afford businesses incorporated there superior lawsuit protection.) For another client I put title to his luxury boat into a limited partnership. Another client has three delivery trucks in a limited partnership owned by his children and his corporation leases the trucks from the limited partnership.

Action Checklist

❑ Review assets that you have titled in joint ownership, in children's names, in the name of a spouse, or as tenants by the entireties.

❑ Consider setting up revocable trusts, or irrevocable trusts, to hold title to these assets. (See Chapter 10, "How Living Trusts Can Protect Your Assets.")

❑ Be sure each of your trusts includes an antialienation clause and a spendthrift clause.

❑ Consider the limited partnership form of ownership for more advanced asset protection. (See Chapter 19, "Limited Partnerships Will Protect Your Assets.")

❑ Review the benefits of corporate ownership in Chapter 18, "The Advantages of Corporations for Businesses and Professionals."

Chapter 10

How Living Trusts Can Protect Your Assets

There are many different types of trusts, and they vary widely in construction and use, but all of them have these characteristics in common:

- A trust contains property.
- The legal and equitable title to the property is divided—that is, though the trust owns the property, the principal and/or income may be disbursed to others.
- The person who holds legal title to the trust property is called the trustee.
- The person who receives the benefit of the property is called the beneficiary.
- The person who creates the trust is the trustor or settlor.
- The person who places the property inside the trust is called the settlor. (The settlor and trustor are almost always the same person.)

- A properly drafted trust will specify the benefits the beneficiary is to receive and the procedures that the trustee must follow.
- Although there are three titles associated with a trust (trustee, beneficiary, and trustor/settlor), one person can have two or even all three titles, though a trust may lose many of its income tax and lawsuit protection advantages when the same person is both trustee and beneficiary.

Living trusts have been touted as a modern-day estate planning miracle, and when set up correctly will avoid probate. Yet while thousands of living trust seminars are given each month across the country, rarely do these seminars discuss what living trusts cannot do. In general, living trusts will not protect your assets from lawsuits or liens. There is, however, one very narrow way in which a living trust will afford you some asset protection.

How a Living Trust Works

In the typical living trust, the husband and wife each must set up trusts into which they transfer their assets, or they set up a joint trust for that purpose. When one of them dies, the disposition of the trust assets is controlled by the terms of the trust itself. Because the will does not govern disposition of those assets, the trust assets bypass probate.

People establish living trusts for some of the following reasons:

- Probate can be avoided on the assets held in the trust.
- Bypass trust and marital trust tax provisions can be placed in the living trust. These provisions provide that assets held in trust for a spouse or child will eventually pass to other heirs, and thus save estate taxes.
- A trust can be revocable, meaning you can amend, alter, or cancel it at any time.
- Through a trust you can appoint competent people or institutions to manage your property during your life or after your death.
- Under some circumstances, trusts can afford a substantial measure of liability protection for the assets they hold (see discussion that follows).
- Irrevocable trusts can provide probate avoidance and income tax advantages while also eliminating estate taxes.
- Unlike a will, a trust is a private document and is not available for public inspection.
- A living trust can go into effect immediately, unlike a testamentary trust, which only goes into effect following death.
- Property can be added to or taken out of the trust at any time.
- A living trust is not generally under the continuing supervision of any court, while a testamentary trust is generally under the continuing supervision of the probate court, requiring periodic accountings to the court that become a part of public record.

Living trusts generally provide no asset protection for the person who sets up the trust. A husband's trust assets can be seized by his creditors, and a wife's trust assets can be seized by hers. Assets held in a joint trust are vulnerable to creditors of either spouse. So, in what sense do trusts protect? Assets in the wife's living trust generally cannot be seized by the husband's creditors, and vice versa, unless fraud can be proved. If the husband is notified of an impending lawsuit and immediately transfers his assets into his wife's trust, the transfer will probably be held to be fraudulent. But if the assets were transferred years before the lawsuit arose, or better yet, were acquired originally by the wife in her own name, fraud will probably not be an issue.

Here is an example of how it works. Look at the following diagram:

WIFE'S REVOCABLE TRUST

HUSBAND'S REVOCABLE TRUST

The diagram indicates that two revocable living trusts have been created. Assuming the husband is a physician and the wife is less vulnerable to lawsuits than he: Many of the family's more valuable assets are placed into the wife's trust. The physician husband's trust contains only a few assets. If a malpractice action is taken against the doctor, the creditors generally can reach only the assets within his trust. The assets in the wife's trust are insulated, unless the conveyance to the wife's trust amounts to a fraudulent conveyance (see Chapter 13, "Surviving Bankruptcy with Your Assets Intact"). In general, the husband may be a cotrustee with the wife over the wife's trust without affecting the reachability of the trust's assets by the husband's creditors.

Living trusts can therefore provide narrow and limited protection if one spouse is vulnerable to lawsuits because of his or her business or professional activities and the spouses acquire their major assets in the name of the nonvulnerable spouse's trust, or if assets already owned are transferred to the trust well in advance of any lawsuits.

Trusts must be set up properly and any transfers to the trusts must be done correctly for the trust to be effective. For example, a husband who wanted to maintain control of all assets made himself sole trustee of his wife's trust and gave himself sole power to revoke the trust or change its beneficiaries. When he later declared bankruptcy, he was shocked to learn that the assets of the trust could be taken by his creditors in the bankruptcy proceeding because he had retained such broad powers over the trust.[1]

The result would have been different if the wife were trustee and had sole power to revoke or amend the trust. Most courts would not allow the husband's creditors to take assets held in the wife's trust if it had existed for some time and was not deemed to be in fraud of the husband's creditors.

In order to use a living trust for limited asset protection, you must generally comply with these procedures:

- Both spouses must convey their assets directly to the less vulnerable spouse's trust.
- Preferably, the less vulnerable spouse is the trustee. The courts will usually allow protection, however, even if the husband and wife are cotrustees.
- The right to revoke or alter the trust in any way belongs solely to the less vulnerable spouse.
- The vulnerable spouse should not attempt to control the operation of the trust in any way, such as having his or her name on the trust checking account.
- The trust files its own income tax return with its own trust identification number or the social security number of the less vulnerable spouse.
- The less vulnerable spouse should demonstrate complete and independent judgment, control, and supervision over all trust assets (for example, open all accounts, sign all checks, and make investment decisions).
- There should be no commingling of the vulnerable spouse's assets with the assets in the less vulnerable spouse's trust.

If both spouses are vulnerable to lawsuits, the living trust will likely give no protection. In Chapter 19, we will discuss what to do if both spouses are vulnerable to suits.

If the spouses subsequently get divorced, the assets placed in living trusts of either spouse are still subject to division, as we discuss in Chapter 14, "How to Protect Your Assets in Divorce."

The Spendthrift Trust

A spendthrift trust is a living trust that is often established by parents with the children as sole beneficiaries. A spendthrift trust has an added provision that allows the trustee to withhold income or principal distributions from beneficiaries. It does so by including a paragraph that says: "The interests of each beneficiary in income and principal shall be free from the control or interference of any creditor of such beneficiary or the spouse of a married beneficiary, or the parent of a child beneficiary, and shall not be subject to attachment or be subject to assignment."

Although the trust is known by the term *spendthrift,* that doesn't mean that your children are wastrels who can't be trusted to use the assets wisely. The main purpose of the spendthrift trust is to protect the assets from dissipation in lawsuits against them. The spendthrift trust can preclude a creditor of either the trustor or the beneficiary from receiving any assets of the trust. For example, a doctor vulnerable to lawsuits conveys his assets to his children's spendthrift trust, with his brother as trustee. When he is sued, the trustee brother can continue making distributions from the trust to the children beneficiaries, leaving the creditors unable to reach the trust assets or income. Also, the children's creditors would be unable to attach assets of the spendthrift trust.

The spendthrift trust must be carefully drafted if it is to render this sort of asset protection. The person setting up the trust should not be the sole trustee. And the trust works best if the person setting up the trust is not also the beneficiary of the trust.

In a Florida case, a mother created a trust for her children, with one of the sons serving as cotrustee. Because the trust had a spendthrift provision, its assets were protected when one of the sons filed for bankruptcy.[2]

The Dangers of Revocability

If the creator of the trust retains the power to revoke or change the trust, that may be sufficient to make the trust assets subject to seizure in many states. In a California case, the courts allowed the creditors to take trust assets where the couple who had set up the trust retained the power to revoke it.[3]

The Irrevocable Trust

A living trust may be revocable or irrevocable. An irrevocable trust is one that cannot be revoked or changed by anyone, including the original trustor, the trustee, or a beneficiary. This type of trust is often created to protect assets from lawsuits against you, or for other gift-giving and estate planning purposes.

Once assets are transferred to the trust, they must remain there and in the control of the trustee. The trustee must follow the original trust instructions regarding distributions to the beneficiaries. For example, an irrevocable trust can be established where the children are the beneficiaries, and the creators of the trust are not entitled to distributions. That would be a special type of irrevocable trust frequently called a "children's trust."

An irrevocable trust is generally not reachable by creditors if it meets these conditions:

- The trustee is independent, such as a bank or a professional person, and not the individual who created and funded the trust.
- The beneficiary is someone other than the individual who created and funded the trust, such as the children.
- The creator of the trust does not retain the right to revoke, amend, or alter the trust.
- Appropriate income and disbursement records are maintained of the trust interests belonging to the children or other beneficiaries.
- The trust is drafted and operated in a businesslike way so as not to appear to be a fraud or a sham, for example, ostensibly owned by the children but in reality owned and controlled by the parents.

Once all the children are of legal age, the trust document may provide that the trust will terminate and all assets can then be conveyed to a family limited partnership where mother and father, as general partners, can control all the assets of the family partnership.

Foreign and Off-shore Trusts

Foreign and off-shore trusts have become popular among some estate planners in recent years. If you transfer control of your assets to a foreign trust, a creditor generally would have to sue in the country where the trust is held to recover any of the trust's assets. These trusts are often created with "flight" provisions that require the trust to be removed to another jurisdiction if there is a lawsuit or other threat against the assets, making it very difficult for the creditor to catch up with the property.

Foreign and off-shore trusts do not offer perfect protection against lawsuits and liens. I met a lawyer at an estate planning meeting in Colorado who said his law firm has now developed the specialty of seizing assets in off-shore trusts, and that they have become quite successful in doing so. And a neighbor of mine who had transferred his home to an off-shore trust was surprised when the Internal Revenue Service seized it anyway and evicted him and his family. The U.S. Supreme Court has ruled that when domestic real estate is involved, the laws of the state in which the real estate is located govern levies and seizures, rather than the law of the foreign country in which the trust is located.

The foreign trust may offer some protection for cash, stocks, and other personal assets, and at the very least will delay and hinder creditors. But don't ignore the potential dangers of foreign and off-shore trusts, including the trouble and expense of having to comply with foreign laws, as well as the potential for loss if a foreign trustee absconds with your fund or a foreign government takes over your assets.

Action Checklist

❑ Hold property in the trust of the spouse least vulnerable to lawsuit. But remember that if you do so you will probably be relinquishing management and control of the property and the ability to make gifts. You may also have diminished your rights in the case of death or divorce.

❑ Transfer property to a trust for the benefit of your spouse or children rather than directly to them.

❑ Don't make the same person both sole beneficiary and sole trustee.

❑ Don't give the beneficiary the right to demand distributions at will.

❑ Include a spendthrift clause in your trust agreements.

❑ Provide that the trustee can withhold distributions from the beneficiary or his or her creditors.

❑ Give the trustee the right to extend the term of the trust so as to prevent creditors from seizing a beneficiary's interest.

Chapter 11

Protecting Your Home from Lawsuits

Martha, a seventy-six-year-old widow, made a serious mistake when she added her son's name to the deed for her home. She knew that she would die someday, and by making him joint owner she intended that the home would go directly to her son, without probate, at her death. She didn't know the perils of joint ownership until a neighbor told her he had learned that her son's creditors were trying to take her home away from her to satisfy the debts her son owed.

The Dangers of Joint Ownership

Thousands of people put their homes into joint ownership each year. If the home is owned jointly by two (or more) people, it will automatically become the property of the surviving owners when one of the joint owners dies. Thus, the cost and delay of going through probate is eliminated. But because a 1985 U.S. Supreme Court decision[1] upheld the right of a creditor to seize the ownership interest of an owner of jointly held property, many people have unnecessarily lost their homes to creditors and other legal seizures simply because title is held incorrectly.

There are other drawbacks to joint ownership, as Susan, a young mother of two, found out. Her widowed father, who had remarried six months earlier, lay dying in a hospital bed. "Don't worry," he assured her. "My will says our family home and other property will go to you. Your stepmother will get a couple of small bank accounts, but that's all. She has money from her first husband's death to see her through." As it turned out, however, Susan inherited very little when her father died. He had placed all of his assets, including the home, into joint ownership with his new wife in an effort to avoid probate costs. Because anything titled in joint ownership goes to the surviving joint owner, the provisions of his will leaving everything to Susan were ineffective. The home in which Susan grew up, which her father had intended she own, now belonged to her father's wife of six months.

Many loved ones are disinherited each year by the inappropriate use of joint ownership. Malpractice suits are now being brought against attorneys who carelessly write wills without reviewing how title to the property is held. And because the will only conveys assets held in the name of the deceased, the will is rendered impotent by joint ownership.

Alternatives to Joint Ownership

As you now know, joint ownership may frustrate your wishes to leave property to someone you love, and joint ownership may render your property vulnerable to the joint owner's lawsuits. In addition, it does nothing to protect your home against loss if you are sued. Here are some alternatives to joint ownership that will afford some protection against suit; each has advantages and disadvantages.

Titling Your Home in Your Spouse's Name

If you are vulnerable to lawsuits, you may decide to title your home in your spouse's name. This is the most elementary form of asset protection in America and the most frequently used. For example, a physician may put his home in his wife's name, so that he won't own it, and therefore won't lose it if he is sued for malpractice.

This tactic does not always work. Some courts have held that the conveyance is ineffective, and the wife is just a constructive trustee for the husband. Thus the house may be seized by creditors or the bankruptcy court. In other cases, courts have held that the conveyance from husband to wife is nothing more than an attempt to avoid creditors, in violation of the Fraudulent Conveyances Act.

Before you use this elementary form of asset protection, consider the consequences if your spouse dies. Your home, which belonged entirely to your spouse, will end up in your spouse's probate estate.

Using a Revocable Living Trust

A living trust is a trust into which you convey your property, retaining all rights during your lifetime to manage or sell the property, or to add property to the trust or remove property from the trust (see Chapter 10, "How Living Trusts Can Protect Your Assets"). Many people mistakenly believe that once their assets are placed in a living trust, the assets are insulated from suits. This is simply not true. All states have statutes and court decisions allowing creditors to seize assets of a debtor that are held within the debtor's revocable living trust.

You can, however, transfer your home to your *spouse's* living trust and thereby frequently protect it from your creditors. In general, the assets of one spouse held in that spouse's trust are not reachable by the creditors of the other spouse. This is an extension of the general principle of law that the separate assets of one spouse belong to that spouse without being subject to claims by the other spouse or claims of the creditors of that spouse. This transfer, however, is open to the same challenge to the conveyance discussed above, that the transfer was fraudulent or ineffective. The longer the home is held in the spouse's trust the greater degree of protection against such challenges. This approach provides the additional advantage that, upon death, assets in the trust will bypass probate.

Using an Irrevocable Trust

Some people place their homes in irrevocable trusts—that is, a trust that can't be changed (see Chapter 10, "How Living Trusts Can Protect Your Assets"). Unlike the revocable living trust, which allows you to sell or remove assets during your lifetime, once you have conveyed your assets to an irrevocable trust, they will remain there under the control of the trustee.

The irrevocable trust is advantageous in that it provides substantial lawsuit protection, particularly if the home has belonged to the irrevocable trust for a substantial period of time before the lawsuit commenced. As a general rule, courts seldom invalidate an irrevocable trust, particularly where the person who created the trust (the trustor) does not also serve as the manager of the assets (the trustee). Instead, the trustee could be the adult children of the trustor or an independent trustee, such as a bank.

Placing Your Home in the Name of Your Children

As we saw in the widow Martha's case, this approach can have tragic results if the child is sued. But if done correctly and timely, this approach does have a substantial degree of asset protection from lawsuits against either husband or wife. Therefore this approach is frequently used where the husband and wife are both vulnerable to lawsuits or liens. This transfer is still subject to an assertion that you have violated the Fraudulent Conveyances Act by transferring the home to the children in anticipation of a pending, imminent, or probable lawsuit. The longer the time span between the conveyance to the children and the action by the creditor, the greater the degree of protection against this assertion.

Note that there is an unappealing possible side effect to a transfer of your home to your children. If your child dies, divorces, or declares bankruptcy, the home may become the property of that child's spouse or creditors.

Using a Corporation

Some people deed their homes to corporations. A corporation is a separate legal entity with shares of stock representing the ownership of the corporation. Shares can be given to children, grandchildren, and other family members or associates. Generally, the husband or wife, or both, will serve as officers and directors of the corporation. Because the house is owned by the corporation, and the stock of the corporation is owned by others, there is a substantial degree of protection for the home itself from the creditors of the husband and wife.

However, if you convey your home to your corporation, you may experience considerable income tax disadvantages. If you continue to live in the house, you may either have to pay rent to the corporation, or you will have taxable income equivalent to the fair rental value of the home you enjoy. If the home is sold, none of the favorable income tax breaks for homeowners will apply, including the right to defer taxes by purchasing a replacement home within twenty-four months and the right to exclude $125,000 of capital gains from taxation if you are over age fifty-five. When the house is sold, the corporation will have to pay income taxes on the gain, and if the cash received from the sale is distributed to you, taxes will have to be paid on that amount again as dividend income to you. In other words, you will be subject to double taxation.

Using a Limited Partnership

Using a limited partnership is an advanced form of asset protection for a home in America today. When used correctly, a limited partnership has superior lawsuit and lien protection because a special statute, called a "charging order," generally prohibits creditors from seizing the assets of a limited partnership. There are some complex rules dealing with business purpose and other requirements with which the draftsman must be intimately acquainted in order to correctly implement the limited partnership, so it is important that the attorney who drafts the documents be an expert in limited partnerships to perfect this protection.

Using Tenancy by the Entireties

Twenty-three states plus the District of Columbia permit a form of ownership between husband and wife known as tenancy by the entireties. Those states include Alaska, Arkansas, Delaware, Florida, Hawaii, Illinois, Indiana, Kentucky, Maryland, Massachusetts, Michigan, Mississippi, Missouri, New Jersey, New York, North Carolina, Oregon, Pennsylvania, Rhode Island, Tennessee, Vermont, Virginia, and Wyoming. Tenancy by the entireties is a form of joint ownership between husband and wife that generally precludes the creditors of one spouse from seizing the assets held in this form, since each spouse is presumed to own the entire asset. This means that tenancy by the entireties provides protection if only one spouse is being sued. However, if both spouses are sued, this form of ownership offers little protection. The laws regarding tenancy by the entireties are gradually changing in many states. Before placing property in tenancy by the entireties, it is important to consult an attorney familiar with this type of ownership to learn the other ramifications that apply in your state.

Dangerous Guests and Visitors

I was invited to speak to the New York Yankees in their clubhouse at Yankee Stadium on the subject of advanced asset protection. One ballplayer told me of a friend, another professional athlete, who lent his home to a relative who threw a wild party. A guest was severely injured at the party and sued the owner of the home, who hadn't even attended the party.

The courts generally hold that if a homeowner knows of a

dangerous condition on his property, then he will be held liable for injuries resulting from this dangerous condition. In some cases, actual knowledge by the homeowner is not even required, if the homeowner *should have* or *could have* known that a dangerous condition existed. For example, in a recent case the court held that a homeowner should have known that a tree in his yard was dead, since the tree had not leafed in years and smaller limbs had been falling off the tree for some time. When a visitor standing on the porch was struck by a large limb that fell off the dead tree, the court held the homeowner liable because he did not use reasonable care to remove the obviously dead and dangerous tree from his property.[2]

Whether or not you will be held liable for injuries to guests at your home generally depends on whether you acted reasonably or negligently. For example, a man who broke his hip in three places when he fell through a hole in the ceiling while helping a friend install ceiling tiles won a suit against his friend, who is probably now a former friend.[3] The suit was won because the homeowner should have known that injury was probable. On the other hand, a housekeeper who was injured while cleaning a chandelier lost her suit against her employers. The court ruled that the homeowners were not negligent in the installation of the chandelier, and that they could not have anticipated that it would fall from the ceiling during the process of cleaning.[4]

The potential liabilities to a homeowner are significant, and every homeowner should carry ample liability insurance on the home. Remember that you can be sued for an amount far greater than your homeowner's insurance policy limits. If you lose the suit, the creditor may be awarded your equity in the home, and may also seize your personal investments, bank accounts, and securities. The least expensive way of augmenting your homeowner's liability insurance is by adding an umbrella liability policy to your insurance coverage. This policy adds an "umbrella" of liability coverage to your homeowner and automobile policies, giving you protection to much higher limits than either of the other policies provides.

The Homestead Exemption

The laws of most states include a homestead exemption that will protect a portion of your home equity from suits or liquidation in a bankruptcy proceeding. Although the primary purpose of the homestead statutes is to place the property designated as a homestead out of the reach of creditors, only two states, Texas and Florida, have laws that provide for unlimited homestead exemptions. All others provide limited amounts of protection, ranging generally from $10,000 to $75,000. If the equity in your home is higher than the homestead exemption for your state, your home may be sold in a legal proceeding, and you will receive only the statutory amount allowed for your homestead exemption.

Action Checklist

❏ If you own your home jointly, consider the alternatives to joint home ownership, such as titling your home in your spouse's name, using a living trust or an irrevocable trust, placing the home in the name of children, using a corporation, using a limited partnership, or using tenancy by the entireties.

❏ Review your homeowner's insurance policy to ascertain the upper limits of your coverage.

❏ Consider augmenting your homeowner's liability insurance by adding an umbrella liability policy to your insurance coverage.

❏ Do not depend on the homestead exemption to save your house if you are facing bankruptcy, unless you live in Texas or Florida, which have unlimited homestead exemptions.

Chapter 12

Selling Property
Without Being Sued

If you think that once you've sold something, the property's defects are no longer your worry, consider the plight of one southern California divorcée. A few months after she sold the home she was awarded in her divorce settlement, the purchaser filed a $300,000 lawsuit against her because of a slight crack in the foundation of which she had been unaware. Even though the hairline fracture was probably insignificant and would not have resulted in problems with the home, her attorney advised her to settle the case for $185,000.

Even the sale of a used refrigerator or automobile can result in a possible lawsuit if the purchaser was unaware of a defect in the property purchased. This is often true even if no specific warranties have been made by the seller as to the condition of the property, and even if the defects were hidden and unknown to the seller.

To protect yourself from hidden defects in property you sell, make full disclosure of all known defects, and include a provision in the sales contract that the purchaser has inspected, or had an expert inspect, the property, and is intimately acquainted with all known or potentially known defects in the property. Though this may not completely protect you, it is far superior to remaining silent on the subject of defects.

If the property you are selling is obviously defective, draw specific attention to the defect and include it as part of the written sales agreement as a "known defect." If you attempt to cover up a defect, you may be liable for any injury that results.

For example, a Michigan couple bought a home from a seller who knew the wood-burning stove had been improperly installed. A year later the home was destroyed by fire. Though the property had been sold on an "as is" basis, the seller was held liable because he had actively concealed and failed to disclose a potentially dangerous condition.[1]

In an Illinois case, a seller was held liable when a basement flooded, because he had covered up evidence of previous flooding by installing new vinyl tile. The court said that he was liable to disclose all facts that were not easily discoverable or observable by a buyer.[2]

An Arizona couple sold a home with a backyard swimming pool. The new owners rented the pool to tenants whose young child fell into the pool and nearly drowned. The previous home owners were sued for not "disclosing" that there was a pool, but they were absolved of liability since they did not conceal the pool, which was readily observable.[3]

Your liability as a seller may extend to second and even

later buyers of the same property. In an Indiana case the court held that the original seller's implied warranty of fitness for habitation extended also to subsequent purchasers of a home because the hidden defects manifested later and were not discoverable by the subsequent purchaser's reasonable inspections.[4]

You must be as cautious in selling personal property as you are when selling real property. A boat owner who had installed a faulty generator was held liable for $3 million in damages when the new owner of the boat and his family died from inhaling carbon monoxide.[5]

The "As Is" Sale

You may be able to limit your liability by including a statement such as "this property is sold as is" or "this property is sold as is with buyer assuming all known or unknown risks." When property is sold, there is an implied warranty that the property is free from hidden defects and fit for the purpose intended. This implied warranty can be waived or limited by the parties involved if the waiver is expressly, clearly, and unambiguously set forth.

For example, an Alabama couple noticed cracks in the walls and uneven floors in the home they purchased two years earlier. Because the contract had an "as is" clause, the court did not allow the couple to recover damages from the seller.[6]

An Illinois man found himself out of luck when he sued the seller for fire damage he discovered in the attic of the home he had purchased. The seller had disclosed that the home was fire-damaged and had given the buyer a $500 credit for any future expense caused by the fire damage. The buyer had made two physical inspections of the property with a realtor, and an "as is" clause was included in the contract.[7]

An "as is" clause may not protect you in certain cases. Some courts have ruled that "as is" clauses are enforceable only when both parties have equal or substantially equal knowledge about the property being sold. For example, a seller of New Mexico property who knew the county intended to put a road through the property sold his property "as is." The seller was held liable because the buyer didn't have equal knowledge about the road that would result in less acreage and substantially diminish the property's value.[8]

In another case a seller sold some property that he represented as well built, though he had owned the home briefly and had only superficially inspected it. When the new owner moved in, he found numerous problems and sued the seller. The court awarded damages to the buyer, concluding that the "as is" clause would not protect the seller for material misrepresentation.[9]

How to Maximize Your Protection Against Potential Defects

If you are selling an asset that could have potential problems, first inspect your property *yourself,* or hire an inspection firm to do so, to become aware of potential defects you may pass on to the buyer. If you find defects, or you are afraid there are undetected problems, consider transferring title to the asset to another entity, such as a limited partnership, corporation, or limited liability company. When the property is later sold by that entity, the potential liability may be restricted to that entity. In addition, clearly state that the sale is "as is," and disclose all known defects. Remember that this does not protect you in all instances, but it is surely better than doing nothing.

Action Checklist

❏ When you sell property, make full disclosure of all known defects, and include a provision in the sales contract that the purchaser has inspected the property for defects.

❏ Do not attempt to cover up a defect; if you do, you may be liable for any injury that results.

❏ Include in your sales agreement a statement that the property is being sold "as is," with the buyer assuming all known or unknown risks.

❏ Insert a clause in the sales agreement that the parties are waiving all implied warranties regarding defects.

❏ If you are considering selling a property that could have potential problems, first transfer title to another entity, such as a limited partnership, corporation, or limited liability company, to attempt to restrict future liability to that entity.

Chapter 13

Surviving Bankruptcy with Your Assets Intact

Each year thousands of people file for bankruptcy or are forced involuntarily into bankruptcy. What do they get to keep after the bankruptcy? The answer can be surprising. Just look at the former governor of Texas, John Connally, who survived bankruptcy along with three other prominent Texas businessmen. They all came through bankruptcy with millions of dollars intact. Planning makes the difference. Proper use of trusts, partnerships, and corporations, as well as knowing when, and how, to make gifts, will determine your ability to survive bankruptcy with your assets intact.

Timing Is Everything

When you or your corporation declare bankruptcy, your financial estate is put in the hands of a bankruptcy trustee. Under federal law, the bankruptcy trustee can unwind, or avoid, any transaction made within ninety days of the filing of the petition for bankruptcy. Even transactions made up to a year in advance of the petition filing can be avoided if the creditor at the time of transfer was an insider, such as an officer or director of the bankrupt corporation; or if the transfer was intended to hinder, delay, or defraud a creditor; or if the transfer was made for less than full value. In addition, each state has a law called the Fraudulent Conveyances or Transfers Act that may have different time frames from the federal laws.

People who plan ahead for bankruptcy are more likely to survive with their assets intact. Those people recognized well in advance that they were vulnerable and had a high probability of bankruptcy because of their business dealings, investment strategies, or type of profession. If you are concerned about your own potential for bankruptcy, don't dismiss it as paranoia. Discuss your bankruptcy fears with a knowledgeable attorney who can help you take steps now to protect yourself later.

For example, if you give your entire estate to your children six months before you file for bankruptcy, such action would likely be considered a "badge of fraud," which is evidence that the motivating factor for your gift was to defraud a creditor. Badges of fraud would also include transfers when a suit is pending or expected, one which greatly diminishes your estate, or one where you can retain control of the property. For example, after finding out that the Internal Revenue Service planned to seize a valuable piece of property, one Indiana taxpayer donated the property to his church.[1]

State courts have drawn up their own lists of badges of fraud, which generally include any of the following kinds of conduct:

- The transfer was to an insider.
- The debtor retained control of the property after the transfer.
- The transfer was concealed.
- The debtor had been sued or threatened with suit before the transfer was made.
- The transfer was of substantially all the debtor's assets.
- The debtor absconded.
- The debtor removed or concealed assets.
- The transfer was for less than fair value.
- The debtor was insolvent or became insolvent as a result of the transfer.
- The transfer occurred around the same time a substantial debt was incurred.
- The debtor transferred the major assets of his business to a second party who then transferred the assets to a third party who has agreed to hold the assets for the benefit of the debtor or the debtor's spouse or children.[2]

Elementary Asset Protection

James and Emily, condominium developers, transferred their million-dollar estate to their children. Years later, when the transferred home, bank accounts, stocks, and bonds had swelled to more than $8.5 million, they were sued and ultimately declared bankruptcy. Though the bankruptcy trustee tried to reach the assets in the children's names, he could not. The court was not willing to void transfers made in estate planning and gifting more than seven years prior to the bankruptcy filing.

Outright gifting to children can be dangerous, and I seldom recommend it, since it puts the children in control. What if the children simply keep all the assets? What if a divorce or death occurs and a child's ex-spouse ends up with the assets? It is often better to use such entities as limited partnerships, corporations, and trusts to make the gifts. The assets are conveyed to the entity, and the ownership of the entity is given primarily to the children. Dad and Mom can become general partners of the limited partnership, officers of the corporation, or cotrustees of the trust (but use caution here), so that they maintain control over the entity that owns the assets. Thus they have retained control over the assets while giving away most of the ownership.

The only assets included in the bankruptcy will be the portion of the entity owned by the debtor. For example, in a recent case, a 30 percent partner in a limited partnership declared bankruptcy. The partnership owned a building that had burned down, and the insurance proceeds had just been collected. The creditors wanted to access those proceeds to satisfy their debts, but they were unable to do so. The court ruled that creditors could reach only the debtor's interest in the partnership, not the partnership assets themselves. Thus the insurance proceeds were not included in the bankruptcy estate.[3]

In another case, a woman who had inherited shares in a corporation from her deceased husband declared bankruptcy. The court ruled that the stock of the corporation was the only interest the bankrupt woman had, and that corporate assets were not a part of her bankruptcy estate.[4]

If you anticipate that bankruptcy could be part of your future, it is important to meet with a competent attorney and other financial advisers who can assist in designing a long-term program to provide substantial legal and ethical protection for your family's assets.

Protecting Your Retirement Assets

For years people have believed that pension and profit-sharing plans are judgment-proof. It now appears that what once appeared as a totally protected, safe haven from any kind of judgment is eroding. We are seeing a shift in the direction of opening up pensions and profit-sharing plans and individual retirement accounts so that they are reachable under certain situations. Child support and alimony cases have already invaded the heretofore sacrosanct protected areas of pensions.

There are ways to insulate qualified pension plans from seizure in states that have no statutory exemption from garnishment. For example, in the pension plan or trust provisions themselves, benefits may be held exempt or subject to an exemption from garnishment by including a spendthrift trust clause. (See Chapter 10, "How Living Trusts Can Protect Your Assets" for a discussion of the spendthrift clause.) Many states are enacting legislation to protect a debtor's retirement or pension funds from the claims of creditors. But in many situations creditors may still reach pension funds despite such state legislation. For example, in California, a creditor may attach that portion of the debtor's pension funds that are above and beyond what is necessary to provide for the debtor's support at retirement, after considering all other resources that are likely to be available for his support. That means that if the debtor has substantial financial resources—such as stocks, bonds, certificates of deposit, rents, royalties, and so forth—or significant earning capacity, his pension funds may be subject to partial or complete seizure.

In Texas, legislation has attempted to completely protect pension funds from the claims of creditors if the plans are in conformity with the Internal Revenue Code and the contribution to those funds is not more than the IRS permits. But if a creditor can show that the pension plan does not qualify under the applicable provisions of the Internal Revenue Code, then the creditor may seize the pension fund. And even if the plan is in compliance and the plan assets cannot be reached, Texas courts have held that the pension fund was subject to garnishment once the debtor received funds from the retirement account.

Nondischargeable Debts

There are certain debts that cannot be discharged in bankruptcy. They include:

- many taxes, fines, and penalties
- debts arising from fraud
- debts due to embezzlement or larceny
- alimony and child support
- debts for malicious or willful injury or drunken driving
- governmental education loans.

Action Checklist

❑ If your business dealings, investment strategies, or profession make you vulnerable to bankruptcy, discuss with a knowledgeable attorney the ways to protect yourself.

❑ Consider transferring assets to other entities, but before you do, carefully review the badges of fraud to make sure you are avoiding such transactions.

Chapter 14

How to Protect Your Assets in Divorce

Although more than half of marriages end in divorce, very few people take steps to prepare themselves financially should the relationship fall apart. A prenuptial agreement signed in advance of the marriage, or a postnuptial agreement signed during the marriage, are basic tools to protect the assets of the spouses when the marriage ends, whether in death or divorce. But more advanced tools are available to protect assets beyond those afforded by the relative simplicity of prenuptial and postnuptial agreements.

Prenuptial Agreements

A couple, each marrying for the second time, entered into a prenuptial agreement. The husband had sizable wealth he wanted to preserve for his children from his previous marriage. The husband died not long after the marriage, and his second wife tried to invalidate the prenuptial agreement. She claimed she was unaware of the full extent of her husband's wealth, and that she didn't really understand the agreement she had signed. The courts upheld the prenuptial agreement, finding that though the wife did not know or understand the details of her husband's financial dealings, his financial success was widely known, and she had sufficient knowledge of his financial affairs to have entered knowingly into an agreement.[1]

Many experts recommend that all couples with sizable assets consider executing a prenuptial agreement. Although prenuptial contracts are not often signed by Americans marrying for the first time, such contracts are becoming more prevalent for subsequent marriages. Prenuptial contracts, sometimes called "antenuptial or premarital contracts," change or limit what would otherwise have been the law governing the ownership of property in the marital relationship, especially upon death or divorce.

The most common use of prenuptial contracts is to protect the wealth of WOOFs (Well-Off Older Folks) against access by the other spouse upon death or divorce. In this era of patchwork families, where children may be his, hers, theirs, or even stepchildren from a former marriage, prenuptial contracts can define the inheritance rights of the various heirs, thus deflecting potential challenges to the will upon the future death of one of the spouses.

A prenuptial contract can also protect the less wealthy spouse, who is surrendering financial security in order to marry. Most commonly, the spouse is giving up alimony income, which terminates upon her remarriage. But she may be giving up a lucrative career as well, as Jane Fonda did when she gave up acting to wed Ted Turner.

Sometimes prenuptial contracts are used to protect the control, management, and ownership of a family business from the prospective spouse, or to clarify the separate or marital nature of certain assets brought into the marriage and to be acquired in the future. A prenuptial contract can also ensure that the laws as they exist in the state where the actual marriage occurs will govern in the event of a divorce, no matter where the couple resides in the future.

If no prenuptial contract exists, upon divorce assets are divided in accordance with state laws. Community-property states divide equally any property acquired during the marriage other than that acquired by inheritance or gift, while common-law states give the courts power to distribute property equitably in divorce. Even in community-property states, appreciation of separate property may be considered marital property, especially if the spouse's efforts contributed to the appreciation. Separate property retitled in both names may convert that property to marital property, and separate property used by both spouses, such as the marital home, may be considered converted to marital property.

There are ways to protect separate property other than by signing a premarital contract. For example, the property could be transferred to an irrevocable trust, but that may result in a loss of control and flexibility. If you transfer the property to an irrevocable trust and retain any benefits or powers—such as the right to receive income or the right to distributions of principal—in divorce, your spouse may be entitled to property distributions or support because of those retained benefits or powers.

Some people have sought protection in a premarital revocable trust, but these do not generally protect assets against division in divorce. If the monied spouse dies, the widowed spouse may have a right to claim a portion of the assets held in a revocable trust under state laws, despite trust provisions that grant no interest to the widowed spouse.

A more drastic solution is to give away one's wealth. Gifts prior to marriage may create gift tax problems, as well as deprive the donor of the use of the asset and its income. If the gift is made in contemplation of divorce, it may be subject to attachment as being in fraud of the spouse's claims against the marital estate, and at best will arouse judicial ire.

A prenuptial contract will generally discuss ownership and sharing of property owned at the date of the prospective marriage and property acquired during the marriage. It may also discuss sharing of income from services of both spouses during marriage, and income and appreciation from property owned at the date of marriage or acquired later. The contract may define gift and will provisions between the spouse and others, and may limit the prospective spouse's right under state law, upon the death of the monied spouse, to set aside the provisions of the will and to claim a portion of the estate assets. The contract may also delineate how much support will be allotted to the prospective spouse during and after marriage, though prenuptial contract clauses that seek to severely curtail or eliminate support entirely have generally been found to be against public policy and unenforceable. A prenuptial contract cannot limit a child's right to support.

In 1984, the Retirement Equity Act gave spouses the right to a survivor benefit in their spouse's retirement plan, so that upon the retired employee's death, the surviving spouse will have continuing income. In order for the spouse to waive his or her right to a survivor benefit, he or she must sign specific waivers within ninety days of the employee spouse's retirement date. If the employee spouse has not yet retired, and the spouse wishes to waive her rights to a survivor benefit that would be payable if the employee dies before reaching retirement age, the spouse must sign the waiver on or after the first day of the plan year in which the employee spouse turns thirty-five. The spouse must also give written consent within ninety days prior to any loans from retirement plans.

A clause in the prenuptial contract stating that the pension is entirely the property of the employee spouse will not generally extinguish the spouse's right to a survivor annuity. An effective waiver must be made by written consent of the spouse, with specific language acknowledging the effect of the consent, notarized and witnessed, and executed within the designated time frames. Although a prenuptial contract is not an effective substitute for any of these waivers that are required to be signed, the prenuptial contract may stipulate that the spouse will sign the paperwork necessary to waive spousal benefits, and will execute the necessary waiver at the required time. For added protection, the prenuptial contract should include a clause stating that if the employee spouse fails to request the waiver, or if the waiver is ineffective for any other reason, and the spouse receives survivor benefits, she agrees to pay those benefits over to the beneficiary designated by the employee spouse.

For a prenuptial contract to be enforceable, it must include reasonable disclosure of the parties' financial condition. It is generally advisable to attach financial statements to the contract as an exhibit, and also to provide for positive affirmation by each spouse of knowledge of the other spouse's financial condition. The contract should be reviewed by attorneys for each spouse, and adequate time should be provided for consideration and review of the document and its provisions. A last-minute "Wagner Agreement" (one that is signed while the Wagner wedding march is playing) may not be enforceable.

The agreement must be fair and reasonable, though some states require only that the agreement not be unconscionable—that is, one which no person in his or her senses would make, and which no fair and honest person would accept. It is best to avoid obviously one-sided agreements. For example, rather than stating that the income earned by each spouse is separate property when it is clear that one spouse is unemployed and will continue to be so, it is better to provide that the income earned by either spouse is marital property to avoid future contest by the inexperienced, nonpropertied spouse. The contract should not encourage divorce, for example, by providing that the spouse will have no rights in any property except upon divorce.

The contract must be in writing, and some states require acknowledgment and attorney certification as well. Recision, however, can be oral, and that oral recision may be confirmed by actions not in accordance with the contract—for example, by taking property in both names or commingling marital and separate property in contravention to terms of the contract. The courts will be reluctant to interfere with prenuptial contracts where it is clear that the parties have been living by them. If any loans are made from a spouse's separate property to the marital unit and then repaid, the repaid funds should not be commingled with other separate funds. In most states, loans from separate property to the marital unit will be considered to be in the nature of a gift, so the marital property used to repay the loan will likely remain marital property, and commingling it with separate property generally should be avoided.

When you write up your prenuptial agreement, include a severability clause that says if any provision of the agreement is invalidated, the rest of the agreement will still remain in force. The written agreement should also state that there are no agreements between the spouses other than those included in the prenuptial agreement. This will preclude one spouse from invoking oral promises that he or she says were made in addition to the written promises contained in the agreement.

If you have entered into a prenuptial agreement, title all assets in the husband's name or trust or the wife's name or her trust, or in both names as tenants in common. Do not use joint tenancy or joint ownership, to avoid potential conflict with the terms of the prenuptial agreement. When property is acquired during the marriage and title taken in joint tenancy, there is a presumption that the property is marital property, to be divided between the spouses. It is possible that this presumption may be so strong as to invalidate some provisions of the prenuptial agreement. If the marriage ends in the death of the monied spouse and the property is held in joint tenancy, the legal conflict will be even stronger. In general, all assets held in joint tenancy will go outright to the surviving joint owner, despite any provisions to the contrary in the prenuptial agreement. That means that the death of one spouse could now invite a lawsuit between the surviving spouse and the children of the deceased spouse. By properly titling assets, you won't run that risk.

Who Gets Gifts, Jewelry, and Collectibles?

Sometimes the most heated discussions in a breakup center around gifts, keepsakes, heirlooms, and collectibles. In general, property acquired by gift or inheritance is the separate property of the spouse who receives it. But if the property is given to the other spouse, or titled in the other spouse's name, that may not be the case. For example, a husband who transferred his real estate to his wife as part of an asset protection scheme was dismayed when she filed for divorce, sold the real estate, and refused to give him any of the proceeds. She claimed the property was a gift, and the proceeds were entirely hers. He claimed the property was still entirely his. The courts disagreed with both of them, and split the proceeds between them.

To protect yourself against future squabbles when the relationship ends, gifts should be memorialized by a simple memo, signed by the giver, for each significant gift, showing that the sole purpose of the gift is for love and affection. And if the asset is transferred for any other reason, a memo detailing that purpose should likewise be prepared and signed by both spouses.

The Importance of Property Settlement Agreements

Marital property generally is divided equally in the nine community-property states (Arizona, California, Idaho, Louisiana, Nevada, New Mexico, Texas, Washington, and Wisconsin). When deciding the division of property in other states, most courts take into account the duration of the marriage, the value of property owned by each spouse, the ages of the spouses, the health of each spouse and competence to earn a living, the contribution of each spouse to the accumulation of the property, the income-producing capacity of that property, and in some states, the actions of each party that contributed to the divorce.

It is difficult to predict the judge's decision as he weighs these factors. In one recent case the marriage lasted only fifteen months, but the wife was awarded 50 percent of the marital property.[2] For this reason, it is important for the parties to try to agree on property issues without resorting to trial. This saves the time of the courts and will reduce the attorney fees that will be incurred in a protracted divorce proceeding. If the spouses can work through their differences and arrive at some kind of equitable agreement, they will generally be better off than if they left the settlement to judicial discretion. Such agreements can be reached through attorney negotiation, discussions between the spouses, or mediation.

Advanced Strategies for Divorce Planning

Advanced divorce planning is possible through the use of limited partnerships. For example, a husband wants to retain control of all property, even if the marriage ends in divorce. He tells his wife that they need to transfer all their marital property into a limited partnership for estate-planning purposes. The husband then becomes the sole general partner of the limited partnership, with the wife and husband, and perhaps the children, as the limited partners. Let's say that the husband and wife each own 40 percent of the partnership and the children own 20 percent. In the event of a divorce, the courts generally are precluded from unwinding the limited partnership and are limited to adjusting the percentages of ownership between the spouses. That means that each spouse will probably own 40 percent of the partnership after the divorce, so what is the tactical advantage of the limited partnership? The husband will remain the sole general partner. After the divorce, as general partner, he is in firm control of all of the assets. He can now take wages and other benefits from the partnership, reducing the income to be divided among the partners. And if the husband has included a clause in the limited partnership allowing him to retain income in the partnership for its reasonable needs rather than paying it out, he has an even greater advantage. With this provision in the limited partnership the husband has the right to distribute little, if any, income to the partners, including his ex-wife. The husband, as general partner, now has full control and management of all the assets and can make all the decisions. The wife's rights are restricted to receiving income if and when it is distributed by the ex-husband. Notwithstanding this approach, which is used by many, courts obviously have the authority to hold that this procedure smacks of "dirty tricks" and could readily determine that such a legal maneuver is equitably unjust and set it aside. Even courts have only so much patience with totally lopsided legal maneuvering.

Advanced applications of irrevocable living trusts are sometimes used to accomplish a similar effect, where one spouse is the trustee and therefore in the controlling position as trustee to the exclusion of the other spouse. A regular C corporation is sometimes used to accomplish a similar effect (see Chapter 17, "How to Establish Superior Business Lawsuit Protection," for an explanation). In this approach, after divorce the spouse in control owns stocks with voting rights and the noncontrolling ex-spouse owns nonvoting stock. In another corporate variation, stock ownership may be equal between the ex-spouses, but one ex-spouse has control in that he has an option to acquire the other spouse's stock.

The Risks of Cohabitation

Many couples cohabit for a period of time without entering into a legal marriage. If you do so, decide in advance how assets should be titled so that if the relationship ends, there will be no misunderstanding as to the intention of the parties.

In a recent Minnesota court case, a couple cohabited for four years, during which time the man used his money to purchase the home in which they lived. The home was titled in joint tenancy with his companion, so when the relationship ended, the woman sued for half of the home. The court ruled that she was not entitled to a portion of the house because there was no written contract between the parties, as was required by cohabitation statutes in Minnesota. But in other states, courts are more inclined to make award of property rights between individuals who have lived together. One companion may bring a palimony suit against a former companion to lay claim to a portion of the assets acquired during the period of cohabitation.

An equally unfair allocation resulted in the case of a southern California woman suing her husband of twenty-seven years for divorce. She had met and moved in with him while she waged a protracted and acrimonious legal battle to divorce her first husband. To avoid further complications in her already bitter divorce, she titled the condominium that she and her lover acquired with joint funds in the name of her lover only. After her divorce, they married and moved to a larger home, renting out the condominium titled in the second husband's name alone. Now, twenty-seven years later, she and her second husband were divorcing. The judge ruled that the home, now within eighteen months of being fully paid for, was the property of the second husband, since it was titled in his name and she could not prove any ownership interest.

The secret to financial survival in the area of cohabitation is to properly title assets acquired during cohabitation to reflect the intentions of the parties. Cohabiting couples should also consider drawing up a living-together document that details their understanding of their respective ownership of property, and should incorporate that agreement into a prenuptial agreement if they later decide to marry.

Action Checklist

❑ When preparing a prenuptial agreement, consider the following:

- Don't include provisions that encourage divorce—that is, that allow a spouse to receive more in a divorce than he or she otherwise would receive.
- Include a severability clause.
- Include a provision that there are no agreements between the spouses other than those included in the prenuptial agreement.

Action Checklist (continued)

• Make sure the agreement is fair and with full disclosure of the financial status of each party.

❑ Consider using limited partnerships, trusts, or corporations to protect separate assets.

❑ Be careful to title assets acquired during the marriage in a way that will not conflict with the prenuptial agreement.

❑ Keep a record of who owns gifts and collectibles.

❑ Be aware of the risks of cohabitation, particularly in titling shared assets, and consider drawing up a cohabitation agreement.

Chapter 15

How to Protect Your Personal Assets When Your Business Is Sued

Few people understand the degree to which they jeopardize their personal assets, even their homes, when they sign for a business loan. A client of mine learned the hard way over twenty years ago, when his bank told him they were sorry to have to seize his personal assets to pay his business loans, as he had been a customer of the bank for years. Like many people, he hadn't realized that his personal assets could be taken to satisfy a business loan. The banks are well aware of their rights, however, and often have borrowers sign loans in their individual capacity as well as corporate capacity, or have guarantors or co-makers such as parents, relatives, or friends who can pledge their own personal assets for the security of the loan.

The Continental Divide of Defense

A great continental divide separates the streams and the rivers flowing to the east and to the west in the United States. Similarly, you must be just as absolute in separating your business and its activities, loans, and obligations from your personal assets, including their obligations. If you do business as a proprietorship, there is no legal separation of the business from the individual. The business owner is personally liable to the extent of everything he or she owns for all liabilities and liens of the proprietorship. Too many individuals operating as proprietorships don't realize that their individual assets are easily reachable by creditors to satisfy the debts of the business.

To separate the business from the personal, set up the business as a corporation, a limited partnership, a limited liability company, or some form of trust. This is the beginning step, a first line of defense for your personal assets.

For example, I have a building contractor client who has one construction business incorporated in Arizona, and another incorporated and doing business in California. A limited partnership owns the equipment he uses in both businesses and leases it to the corporations.

People who set up one corporation both to operate the business and to own all its real estate and equipment will be shocked to find that when the business is sued they can lose not only the business but also the real estate, equipment, inventory, supplies, and everything associated with the business.

I have continually told clients over the years to begin in the very early phases of their businesses to organize correctly. Don't wait until a lawsuit or litigation arises before you correctly structure your business or profession.

Piercing Your Business Structure

Even if you set up your business correctly and have it clearly separated from personal asset ownership, the entity itself can be pierced or penetrated—and liability imputed to the individuals involved in the business—if you don't pay careful attention to legal details during the operation of the business.

Just having a corporation is not sufficient. You must operate the corporation correctly and pursuant to the respective state laws. Be sure you have the annual shareholder's minutes as well as the minutes from regular board of directors meetings, that you acquire business licenses in the name of the corporation, and that you file all local, state, and federal tax returns in the name of the corporation. Advertising and promotion must be done in the name of the corporation. Meet with your attorney each year to review all procedures of the corporation to be sure you are complying with the required state laws so that you will be considered in all circumstances to be acting as a corporation.

In a recent case a physician and his wife owned an incorporated clinic and hospital. A patient suffered severe injuries during medical procedures. The court found that there had been substantial commingling between the corporate activities and the personal activities of the directors of the corporation. This decision was reached because money from the corporation was used for personal expenses rather than first taken out as salary. The doctor drove the corporation's automobile for extensive personal use, and he also used his personal residence at times as a clinic. Because of the failure to separate the business from the personal, the doctor and his wife were personally held liable for this lawsuit.[1]

In another case, extensive commingling resulted in the creditors of the corporation being allowed to reach the assets of the individual owner in addition to also reaching the assets of the corporation.[2]

The owner of a small ski hill operated the lucrative venture as one big family business. Everything went into one big pot, and all expenses, including personal expenses, were paid from the common account. When hard times hit, the bankruptcy trustee attached the personal property of both the husband and the wife. This was possible because the assets and expenses of the individuals were so commingled with the business assets and expenses that they were indistinguishable from the corporate assets.[3]

Consider setting up a one-person corporation, where only one member of the corporation is appointed president, secretary, incorporator, and director. This is a rapidly evolving approach to structuring corporations in lawsuit-prone businesses, and in this way you can limit the individual liability exposure of those who are actively involved in the business. Other family members can be involved in the business as employees, or even stockholders, without significant liability exposure.

As you structure your business or profession, always consult with an expert who will help you cleanly, lawfully, and properly separate the business from your personal activities and your personal holdings.

Successful Separation

If you set up a corporation and operate it correctly, paying attention to corporate details, then negligent acts associated with the corporation generally will not allow your individual assets to be reached.

In one case, the president of a corporation who signed a contract with the U.S. government to perform janitorial services was not held liable when the corporation breached the contract. The court said that he could not be held liable for the corporate debts merely because he was an officer of a corporation.[4]

In another case, when a creditor of a corporation came after the shareholders personally, the court held that the creditor would have to prove that the corporate formalities were not followed, or that there was a commingling of corporate and personal funds so as to disregard the separate corporate entity. In this case the court observed that the husband and wife shareholders did follow the corporate formalities and did act as a corporation, so the creditor was precluded from going after the couple's personal assets.[5]

How Personal Assets Can Be Correctly Used by a Business

Businesses usually need real estate, equipment, and other assets readily available. To protect those assets, it is often best that they not be owned by the business. Frequently, assets such as real estate or equipment will be owned by a separate corporation, a limited partnership, a trust, or even individually by the owner of the corporation. *This separate ownership and its lease back to the business corporation should be very clearly documented.*

For family-owned businesses, I often recommend that the parents and children own as a limited partnership the building and land used in a business. Perhaps the children or grandchildren can own the equipment through the use of a children's trust, also known as a Sec. 2503(c) trust. Regardless of which entity is used to hold title to the real estate or equipment, this entity must in every instance enter into a written lease with the corporation for the use of the land, the building, or the equipment. I have never seen a court allow the creditors of a corporation to seize assets owned and leased in this manner. There is no substitute for clearly delineating ownership of the major assets by an entity other than the business corporation.

The overall protection of your home and other personal assets from reachability by a business creditor depends largely on how you hold title to those assets. If the correct legal entities are utilized for those assets, then business creditors are generally prohibited from reaching and seizing those assets.

Here is an example of how we protected the assets of an attorney who was a client of our law firm, by creating critical separation between his business and personal assets.

First of all, we incorporated his law practice, but we did not put any significant assets into the name of the corporation. We could have used a Limited Liability Company or a Limited Liability Partnership in place of a corporation. Then we transferred his office equipment, computers, desks, furnishings, art, and decorative items into a Limited Partnership. The attorney, as general partner, owned 1 percent of the partnership, and the rest was owned by his wife and two children, ages eight and twelve, who were limited partners.

The Limited Partnership negotiated a one-year equipment

lease with the Professional Corporation, which allowed the Professional Corporation use of the equipment and furnishings in exchange for a lease payment. Because the lease was for just one year, rather than three years or more, the Professional Corporation was able to take a larger tax deduction for its lease payments to the Limited Partnership, so the attorney was able to shift substantial revenues from the law practice to the children, via the Limited Partnership. In addition, the equipment, furnishings, and Limited Partnership revenue are all insulated from a malpractice lawsuit and judgment against the attorney or his Professional Corporation.

Having taken care of the business property, we now turned our attention to the attorney's personal assets. To protect them from loss in the event of a large malpractice judgment against the attorney, we put the family home in the wife's Revocable Living Trust. (Although few courts would attempt to seize the home from the wife if the husband was sued, some attorneys would recommend conveying the home to a Limited Partnership or Limited Liability Company for added protection.) To protect the rest of the attorney's assets, we conveyed his stocks, bonds, mutual funds, a vacant lot, and a rental home that he owned to a Limited Partnership.

If you operate a business from your home, you can still successfully separate business and personal assets. I have a client who runs a lucrative Amway business from his home. We structured the Amway business as a corporation, and transferred the home and a few other assets to a Limited Partnership. The Limited Partnership then leased a room in the home to the Amway corporation. We created a trust for the children, and transferred the business equipment and computer into the Children's Trust, for the benefit of the three children, ages fourteen, sixteen, and seventeen. The Children's Trust then leased that equipment to the Amway corporation on a short-term lease, which allowed the Amway corporation to deduct the lease payments, thus transferring income from our client to the children, to be taxed at their lower tax brackets. Note that this would not have been as effective a strategy if the children were younger, as children younger than fourteen pay tax on most of their income at their parents' tax rate.

No matter what your business or profession, you can structure a legal, effective separation of the business from the business assets and your other assets and investments. This separation is critical for total asset protection.

Action Checklist

❑ To separate your business from your personal life, set up the business as a corporation, a limited partnership, a limited liability company, or some form of trust.

❑ To protect your assets, set up your business correctly from the very beginning rather than waiting until a lawsuit threatens.

❑ Adhere to all the legal technicalities in setting up and operating your corporation so as to protect the corporate structure from being pierced.

Action Checklist (continued)

❑ Consider setting up a one-person corporation, with the same person as president, secretary, incorporator, and director.

❑ Do not commingle personal and corporate funds, or utilize corporate assets personally.

❑ Consult with an expert who will help you separate the business from your personal activities and holdings.

❑ Put business assets into a separate legal entity, such as a limited partnership trust, or give them to your children.

❑ Have the corporation sign a lease with the owner of the business real estate and equipment, and adhere to the formal requirements of the lease.

Chapter 16

Choosing the Best Insurance for You

When you're considering insurance coverage for yourself, read the fine print for technicalities that let insurance companies walk away from coverage. That lesson was learned the hard way by a midwestern man I met a few years ago at a conference. He told me of a terrible accident that happened at the apartment building he owned. A tenant's guest stepped out onto a second-floor deck, then leaned over the railing to get a better view. Because of some rust damage, the railing gave way and she fell to the pavement below. Her injuries left her in a vegetative state, and her family filed suit against the building owner. Although the owner was unaware that the railing had a rust problem, he was in violation of a local ordinance requiring metal balconies to be maintained free of rust. The fine print in his insurance policy said there was no coverage if there was a violation of any local or community ordinance. Because of this ordinance violation, the insurance company was able to wiggle out of coverage, leaving the building owner uninsured and vulnerable to the legal onslaught and financial destruction that ensued.

In another incident, a client and his friend had been four-wheeling through sand dunes outside Palm Springs. The vehicle flipped and severely injured the passenger, leaving her a quadriplegic. She filed suit. Her friend was confident he had ample auto and homeowner's insurance to cover any award, but he was wrong. Both policies excluded from coverage accidents related to off-road vehicles.

Insurance has traditionally been the primary line of defense against legal attacks. However, this line of defense is no longer adequate. First, the cost of insurance has gone up tremendously and the amount of coverage available has decreased. Second, the average lawsuit award continues to climb. Thus, more and more often awards exceed the insurance policy limit. Finally, when a person makes a claim against his insurance policy, he often finds that his insurance premiums go up substantially or that the company cancels the policy altogether, or that his claim is not covered by the policy due to some well-drafted exception provision in the policy.

Finding the Right Insurance Company

To find reputable insurance agents, ask your friends, neighbors, and business colleagues for recommendations, then interview at least three insurance agents. Be sure to include independent agents, who sell policies from several different companies, as well as agents who work for just one insurance company. Describe your family situation and insurance needs to each agent, listen carefully to their recommendations, and compare prices. You may also wish to consult periodic surveys published by *Consumer Reports* of customer satisfaction with insurance companies. After you have selected your insurance, each year meet with two insurance agents to review the policies you now have to seek their recommendations and compare their prices.

It is important to have the right coverage and enough coverage. But it is just as important that your insurance be purchased from a company with financial staying power. After hurricane Iniki struck Hawaii, three of the major insurers in the islands collapsed. Allstate Insurance dropped 300,000 Florida homeowner policies after its staggering losses from hurricane Andrew. Even Lloyd's of London, the bulwark of the insurance industry, has suffered crippling losses in recent years.

How can you find a reliable insurance company with adequate financial strength? To maintain maximum security, buy only from insurance companies that have an A++ rating from A. M. Best, the company that rates the financial health of insurance companies. Your insurance agent can give you information from A. M. Best and other independent rating services. For a modest fee, you can request a rating report on an insurance company through Weiss Research, Inc., of West Palm Beach, Florida, (800) 289-9222.

Many state statutes require insurance companies to create a fund from which to pay claims in the event an insurance company in the state becomes insolvent. Even if your state provides such pooled coverage, you should still exercise care in choosing an insurance company. If your insurance company fails, the fund may not protect you completely, since it is obligated to pay claims only to the extent provided by state statute. Although you may have paid premiums for extended coverage, bare-bones reimbursement for your basic losses may be all you get. For example, your auto policy may provide for car rental reimbursement and towing charges, but the state statute may provide for nothing more than repairs to your damaged vehicle.

What Kind of Insurance You Need for Lawsuit and Asset Protection

Automobile Insurance

Be sure the liability portion of your auto policy is large enough. If you've had the same coverage for years, it is probably time to increase your liability coverage. Few people should have less than $100,000 of coverage, and many should have $1 million or more coverage per accident. To play it safe, your liability coverage should approximate your net worth, so that if you are sued for all you are worth, the insurance company will have to ante up rather than you.

Homeowner's Insurance

This is essential. Consider adding liability coverage up to a million dollars or more in your policy. It is relatively inexpensive and well worth it.

Not all homeowner's insurance policies are alike. Many people maintain fire and extended coverage insurance on their homes. That type of insurance is relatively inexpensive, but there are many casualties it does not cover. Consider spending a bit more and upgrading your coverage to the all-risk form of the homeowner's policy, which extends coverage for a broad range of casualties.

Exceptions to Coverage. There are varying interpretations by insurance companies and courts as to what losses are covered. For example, a homeowner was shocked when a neighbor's faulty plumbing system flooded his basement. He was stunned to learn that his insurance did not cover "water damage below the exterior surface in elevation of the home," which meant that the extensive damage to his basement was uninsured.[1]

An Arizona woman providing baby-sitting services in her home went into the backyard to feed her dog. A child climbed onto a picnic table and fell, suffering serious injuries. The woman's insurance company refused to pay, citing a clause that stated injuries "related to a business pursuit" were excluded from coverage under her policy.[2]

Umbrella Liability Insurance

This is possibly the most important insurance policy you can have. You can add an additional and broader liability coverage to your existing policies that greatly expands the total amount of your liability coverage and your increased premium may be very small. An umbrella policy expands the liability coverage to areas not covered by traditional home and auto policies, guarding you from a lot more liability situations than a normal homeowner's or automobile policy. For example, an umbrella policy provides insurance protection if you are sued for defamation, slander, or libel. Umbrella insurance is extremely valuable, but it isn't expensive, and costs just a few hundred dollars a year for several million dollars worth of protection.

The Oelhalfen family of Wisconsin will forever be grateful for their umbrella coverage. When a judgment of $925,000 was awarded against them for an accident in their boat, their primary policy paid only to its $500,000 limit. But their umbrella policy paid the additional $425,000, saving them from bankruptcy.[3]

There are two kinds of umbrella policies: one for personal liability, and one covering business liability. Be sure to talk to your insurance agent about expanded coverage, both personally and for your business.

As you compare prices for the different types of insurance you need, be sure to ask if you would save money by placing your automobile, homeowner's, and umbrella liability policies with the same insurer to obtain a quantity discount.

Malpractice and Errors and Omissions Insurance

Malpractice insurance, often known as errors and omissions insurance, protects a professional or business owner from mistakes he or she makes in a business capacity. This type of insurance is a must for professionals and business owners, but remember that lawsuits often exceed policy limits, so review the needed amount with your carrier frequently.

Medical Insurance

To protect your assets, you must have a major medical insurance policy with a high upper limit of coverage. I learned that in the early years of my law practice, when I met clients who had suffered the consequences of ignoring this advice. This man and his wife, both in their late forties, had built a moderate estate and were building a secure retirement nest egg when their teenaged daughter developed a brain tumor. After an expensive surgery, the tumor continued its rapid growth, and six months later she was in surgery again. After a third surgery two years later, the medical bills had exceeded two million dollars, and the couple was broke. Their basic health insurance covered only a fraction of the cost, and the couple lost their entire estate paying for their daughter's medical costs. Amazingly, a major medical policy with a high upper limit may be relatively inexpensive if it has a high deductible. The policy I carry has a $10,000 deductible, and it costs little compared to a policy that pays for every doctor call.

How Much Insurance Is Enough?

Life Insurance

Life insurance coverage is important in order to provide cash for expenses when you die. Review your insurance needs carefully every few years to be sure your insurance coverage is adequate, and that you are not over- or underinsured. I met a ninety-two-year-old woman who purchased a $1,000 life insurance policy in the late 1920s. She was assured by the insurance agent that the policy would provide enough money for her burial and considerable additional income for her family. The salesman didn't tell her about the effects of inflation on the value of the policy, and she struggled over the years to pay the premiums on a policy the benefits of which provided ever-shrinking buying power.

When I was a recent college graduate with a young family, my neighbor Gary and I compared insurance premiums. I showed him my term insurance policy that provided $150,000 of annual coverage, and he scoffed. "Look," he said, "I'm paying the same amount of premiums for $10,000 of coverage, but my policy is building cash value every year that I can use

for retirement. All you have at the end of each year is a can-
celed check, and a term policy that has expired." Six months
later, my wife and I visited Gary as he lay in a hospital room
dying of cancer. Gary's widow and children struggled for
years because of Gary's improper insurance planning. This
experience has etched in my mind the importance of providing adequate insurance for your family's future needs before
you begin to build an estate to fund your retirement.

Liability Insurance

What happens if you are hit with a judgment that exceeds
your insurance coverage? The judgment creditor will then go
after any assets you have: house, car, boat, pension plan, savings, real estate, and other investments. Judgments seem to
be getting bigger and bigger. In today's litigious world, how
much insurance do you need? To compute the right amount,
just multiply your shoe size by your social security number.
But joking aside, the day is gone when a few hundred thou-
sand dollars of liability insurance is enough. Massive judgments are awarded as judges and juries grapple with the
question of the potential value of a human life. As a minimum,
you need a million dollars of liability insurance. Many people
should carry $5 million to $10 million of insurance to protect
themselves against financial disaster. If you are underinsured, before you turn to the next chapter, call your insurance agent to increase your coverage. It is well worth the
investment.

Never rely solely on insurance protection, because it might
not cover you in a given situation. Learn how to protect and
insulate your personal assets as a backup in case of inadequate coverage by your insurance company.

Action Checklist

❑ Choose an insurance company that has financial staying power.

❑ Consider placing your automobile, homeowner's, and umbrella liability policies with the same insurer to obtain a quantity discount.

❑ Opt for all-risk insurance for your real estate.

❑ Purchase at least $1 million of umbrella liability insurance, and consider $5 million to $10 million of coverage.

❑ If applicable, purchase errors and omissions coverage or malpractice insurance.

❑ Review your insurance coverage with your agent at least every five years.

❑ Purchase a major medical insurance policy that provides several million dollars of upper-limit coverage, even if you must opt for a high annual deductible amount in order to afford the premiums.

❑ When your family is young, purchase enough term insurance to cover their continuing needs before you begin building your retirement funds.

Part II

How to Protect

Your Business

Assets

Chapter 17

How to Establish Superior Business Lawsuit Protection

Who would ever imagine that running out of gas could place the owner of a business in danger of bankruptcy?

It happened to Tom, who owned a small unincorporated farming business. He sent his employee to a neighboring town to get supplies, and on his way back to the office in the company car, the employee ran out of gas. He coasted the car to the side of the road and left it there, unaware that the left side of the vehicle protruded a foot into the main traffic lane. A few minutes later a vacationing couple slammed into the rear of the abandoned vehicle, killing the husband instantly. The wife died a few hours later.

Unfortunately, the insurance on the vehicle had expired, so when a wrongful death action resulted in a massive suit against Tom, the business owner, he was forced into bankruptcy by a judgment that exceeded his insurance coverage.

Stories like this are repeated all over America every day. People often lose everything because they fail to correctly establish their businesses. Had Tom's business been incorporated, the corporation would be considered the employer, not Tom, and generally only assets held by the corporation would have been used to pay the judgment.

The Time Factor

Timing is everything when it comes to incorporating. I met with a new client who was in a hurry to incorporate his business; his employee had been responsible for a serious accident in the company car that morning. I had to advise him that he was one accident too late to benefit from the limited liability protection a corporation offers. He needed to have his business up and running as a corporation before the accident occurred.

The Five Forms of Doing Business

There are five major business entities used in this country: proprietorships, general partnerships, limited partnerships, corporations, and limited liability companies. Here are the pros and cons of each.

Proprietorships

Generally, a proprietorship has no lawsuit or liability protection other than the insurance it carries. Though it is a common way of transacting business, the proprietorship is one of the riskiest business structures around. Whenever tax liability or a lawsuit occurs, the liability will be imposed personally on the owner.

Liability may also extend to the owner's spouse, because the courts often treat the proprietorship as a constructive partnership. If the spouse is participating in the management or the decision-making process of the business, the owner and the spouse will be sued under the theory that both of them are responsible for the business.

I believe that the proprietorship is too dangerous a structure for most people to use. Too often, people lose everything when their proprietorship is sued.

General Partnerships

A general partnership is an association of two or more people in a business or professional venture with a view to making a profit. The dangers lurking in a general partnership or an unwritten joint venture can exceed the dangers of a proprietorship. In a general partnership, if one partner acting on behalf of the partnership does something wrong, liability also generally attaches to the innocent partners.

In addition, general partners are not protected from lawsuits against the general partnership. A group of four doctors involved in a real estate development learned this lesson the hard way. Before the development was finished, they amassed over $5 million in lawsuits and judgments against the partnership. Each doctor was held to be individually liable for the full amount because of the general partnership form of business. As do many people, the doctors had spent too much time thinking about how profitable their new business would be, and not enough time concentrating on the preventative steps they needed to take to ensure that they had maximum liability protection.

Limited Partnerships

Limited partnerships, if set up correctly, provide substantial limitations of liability. Limited partners are generally not held liable for the acts of the partnership as long as they do not actively participate in the management. The general partner is usually liable, as is the partnership itself.

My neighbor formed a limited partnership to own an apartment project in Arizona. He served as general partner and his children were limited partners. Subsequent litigation resulted in a judgment against both the limited partnership and the general partner. Because his children were limited partners, they were neither sued nor held personally liable for the obligations of the limited partnership.

Corporations

The corporate form of doing business provides superior lawsuit protection because the corporation is considered a separate "individual" with the same rights, duties, and obligations as any individual. That means that the corporation can sue and be sued in its own right.

To preserve the legal separation of the corporation from the owners, officers, and directors, it is not sufficient merely to select the corporate form of organization. You must fully comply with all requirements in running the corporation, including holding the initial organizational meeting, regular board of directors meetings, and annual shareholders' meetings. In addition, you must properly set up the corporation by adopting corporate bylaws, issuing corporate stock, getting the proper state and local business licenses in the corporate name, transferring assets to the corporation, advertising and serving notice that the business is now operating as a corporation, maintaining proper accounting records and up-to-date corporate records, and filing annual state and federal report forms.

One of the most common mistakes that I see is the commingling of corporate and personal assets. This frequently occurs where the corporation purchases business assets that are then used by the officers, directors, shareholders, or employees—for example, an officer takes a video recorder from the business and uses it at home. Acts of this nature can allow creditors to pierce the corporate veil and sue the individuals behind it, arguing that a valid corporation does not exist.

There are two types of corporations, an "S" corporation and a "C" corporation. An "S" corporation, formerly called a "Sub-Chapter S" corporation, pays no income taxes. As with a partnership, the "S" corporation's income is passed through to the shareholders, who pay taxes on the income at their tax brackets. Unlike the "S" corporation, the "C" corporation pays taxes on its net income, after deducting salaries and other deductible business expenses. In general, both types of corporation have superior lawsuit protection, because both entities are legal corporations, and hence afford the full protection of state law for corporations and shareholders. You and your adviser should make the decision as to which type of corporate status is best for you by analyzing the tax benefits of each.

Professionals will often create corporations to protect themselves from the acts of an associate. For example, if three doctors each have their own corporations, in general, one doctor won't be sued personally for the act of another doctor. The same would be true even if the three doctors form only one corporation, with each owning one-third of the stock of the corporation.

Sometimes, multiple corporations are created to increase

liability protection. For example, one of my clients, a soft-drink manufacturer, used one corporation to bottle and sell the soft drinks, and another corporation to operate the fleet of trucks that delivers the soft drinks.

Limited Liability Corporations (LLCs)

The use of limited liability corporations is a growing trend throughout America. Wyoming was the first state to authorize this business form in 1977, and many more states have since followed suit. The LLC is a hybrid entity that possesses both corporate and partnership characteristics. It shields its officers and members from the liabilities and lawsuits of the enterprise, but generally is treated as a partnership for income tax purposes.

Because the LLC is a relatively new entity, there is not as much case law concerning this business form. Therefore, for many years to come, there will be lawsuits brought before the courts to challenge the LLC as a lawsuit protection device. Even so, if the LLC is allowed in your state, you should consider its superior lawsuit protection for your business.

Summary

The corporation is a generally optimal business form for superior lawsuit protection. Corporations require expenses such as filing fees, attorney fees, and accounting fees, but most business owners will find the lawsuit protection well worth it. If unincorporated, they flirt with disaster. The proprietorship provides you with no protection. In a general partnership, the general partners can be sued along with the partnership, and one partner can be held liable for the wrongful acts of another partner. Limited partnerships can be used for many business activities, but in most cases they fall short of the advantages found in the corporate structure. Limited liability corporations are new and relatively untested, but will probably provide superior lawsuit protection in future years.

Action Checklist

❑ Consider the five entities listed previously for each of your businesses and determine which ones are appropriate for you.

❑ Ask your adviser the following questions:

• Should I incorporate my business now, even though I don't need to for income tax purposes? (Keep in mind that the decision to incorporate isn't purely a tax decision. Many businesses should incorporate solely for lawsuit protection reasons.)

• Should I select the "S" form or the "C" form of incorporation?

• Is a limited partnership appropriate for my business?

• If I am a professional working with other professionals, should each professional set up a separate corporation, or should we operate together in one corporation?

• Which state should I incorporate in? (Many businesses now incorporate either in Delaware or in Nevada because of superior statutory protection for corporations.)

Action Checklist (continued)

• Should I use multiple corporations for my business? (For example, one corporation can operate the business headquarters, another can hold the real estate assets, and another can hold equipment and other assets. This approach is often used so that a lawsuit against one entity will not trigger the loss of assets in the other corporations.)

• Which assets should the corporation own, and which assets should be owned outside the corporation so that a lawsuit against the corporation will not result in the loss of those assets?

• In a family-owned business, should I use a one-person corporation so that potential liabilities will not be passed on directly to the members of the family? (Many people set up a corporation with the husband serving as president, secretary, sole incorporator, and the only director. Other family members could be shareholders without creating personal liability exposure for themselves.)

• If I continue to operate in a partnership, what steps must I take now to protect my personal assets so that if my partner does something wrong, I won't lose everything if I, too, am sued? (Remember that, in general, all part-

Action Checklist (continued)

ners can be sued for the act of only one of the partners.)

• If allowed in my state, should I consider creating a limited liability corporation at this time, or is it so new and unpredictable that it is better to wait until the courts render more favorable decisions?

• If I have two separate businesses, should I set up two separate corporations or only one corporation? (In general, two separate corporations often afford more lawsuit and liability protection.)

Chapter 18

The Advantages of Corporations for Businesses and Professionals

How Proper Use of a Corporation Provides Protection

The corporation is the dominant business structure in America. Corporations account for 88 percent of the gross receipts of all business entities.

Attributes of Corporations

Here are some of the attributes of the corporation:

Legal Entity.   A corporation is a legal entity separate from its shareholders. The rights and liabilities of a corporation are completely distinct from those of its shareholders. Title to corporate property is held by the corporation, not the shareholders. Even when one person owns all the stock, he is separate from the corporation.

Created by Statute.   You can form a corporation only by complying with a state's incorporation statute. All states have them, but they vary. Some state statutes offer more advantages than others. (See Chapter 20, "Which States Give the Best Lawsuit Protection," for a discussion of this.)

Limited Liability.   Because a corporation is an entity separate from its shareholders, its liabilities are paid from its own assets. Thus shareholders are generally not personally liable for corporate debts and actions beyond the amount of their own investment. Also important, a corporation is not liable for the personal obligations of its shareholders.

Free Transferability of Corporate Shares.   With some exceptions, shares in corporations may be transferred by gift or sale. Of course, free transferability can be contractually altered, for example, by requiring shareholders to sell shares back to the corporation or to each other.

Perpetual Existence.   A corporation exists as an entity for an unlimited duration unless a limited time period is prescribed in the Articles of Incorporation. This allows officers, directors, and shareholders to change while maintaining the corporation intact.

Centralized Management.   The shareholders elect a board of directors who in turn are responsible for managing the company. They declare dividends, authorize major corporate contracts, issue authorized shares of stock, and recommend changes in the corporate charter or bylaws. The board of directors also appoints officers to handle the day-to-day operations of the corporation. Neither the directors nor the officers need to be shareholders of the corporation, though they frequently are.

Rights as a Person. In many circumstances, state and federal law treats the corporation as a person. For instance, a corporation enjoys certain constitutional protections. These include Fifth and Fourteenth Amendment rights to due process, Fourteenth Amendment rights to equal protection, and Fourth Amendment freedoms from unreasonable search and seizure. However, corporations do not have Fifth Amendment rights against self-incrimination.

When a Corporation Is Necessary

Many professionals don't believe the protection of a corporation will benefit them, since they can't hide behind corporate immunity for suits by their patients or clients. But there are many other suits not related to professional services for which a corporation may give protection. For example, a California doctor who attended my seminar said he wished he had heeded my advice. He fired an employee who filed an action against him for wrongful termination of employment. He now has a $250,000 personal judgment against him. If he had incorporated his professional practice, the lawsuit judgment would most likely have been rendered against the corporation rather than against the physician himself. Similarly, a professional can use a corporation to protect himself from liability for clients or guests injured on the business premises, since such injuries usually do not arise from personal acts of the professional.

Here are some situations that might signal the need for a corporation:

- You are involved in a business where you have one or more employees.
- You are involved in a business or profession where you frequently interact with people, clients, patients, or other businesses.
- You are involved in joint ventures with others in which you might be held jointly or severally liable for any misfortunes of the joint venture.
- You are involved in potentially hazardous situations (for example, you are a contractor, excavator, etc.).
- You are one of two or more professionals who practice together or even share office space in which the physical layout of the space could give reasonable inference to the public that you are in a partnership.

Lawsuit Protection

For most people, the best business structure is a corporation because of the added lawsuit protection they receive. Many professional corporations are being established to afford liability protection for the practicing professionals from the potential negligent acts of their employees and each other. All states have a professional association act that allows the practice of certain professions by properly licensed professionals under corporate structures. An underlying purpose of these acts was to allow professionals certain corporate and tax advantages not allowable to individuals or partnerships. Often, if five doctors are practicing together, I recommend that each doctor has his or her own separate professional corporation, and that they then practice together as a general partnership of five professional corporations. In other instances, I will create only one corporation and each of the five doctors will be shareholders. Both situations provide substantial liability protection; the determination of whether to have five corporations or one corporation is usually based on the relative income tax consequences.

Generally, under the corporate structure, if one of the five doctors commits malpractice, the patient can sue the corporation and the doctor who caused the injury, but generally the other four doctors will not be sued. In order to sue and obtain a judgment against the other four doctors, the patient would have to prove that each doctor's actions were negligent with respect to his treatment. Doctors, attorneys, or other professionals belonging to the same professional corporation are not automatically liable for each other's acts of negligence, as would usually be the case in a general partnership, and thus their personal assets would be insulated.[1]

In an interesting case, a nurse anesthetist employed by a professional service corporation was negligent, and the court ruled that because the nurse had acted independently and had not been under direct supervision by any of the doctors, the doctors could not be held personally liable for their employee's acts.[2]

In order to gain asset protection, you must not only form a corporation but you must also *act* as a corporation and not a partnership. You must comply with corporate formalities, such as issuing stock, maintaining minutes of director and shareholder meetings, filing corporate tax returns, and identifying your business as a corporation in advertising, on letterhead, and in all other dealings with the public. It is also important to keep your corporation and your personal life separate. Personal funds and other assets should not be mixed with corporate funds, and corporate property should not be diverted to personal use. To avoid liability for corporate debt, don't sign personal guarantees on behalf of the corporation. If you, a family member, or another entity owned by you has dealings with your corporation, make sure they are well documented and at arm's length. And keep your corporation strong with adequate capitalization, so the corporate structure can't be pierced by someone claiming that it is merely a veil for your personal activities. If you fail to look and act like a corporation, the court could overlook the corporate form and determine rights and liabilities of your business according to partnership law rather than corporation law.[3]

If you set up multiple corporations, have different ownership mixes and different directors and officers for each corporation. Use different business locations and employees for each corporation, and have each corporation pay its own debts. If you maintain these distinctions among your corporate entities, you will avoid the possibility that someone will be able to collect a judgment against one of the corporations from the assets of another by claiming that the corporations are separate in name only.

Be aware that a corporation cannot insulate you from your own individual professional negligence. Most states have statutes that specifically maintain personal liability. These statutes are designed to prevent doctors, lawyers, and other professionals from avoiding personal liability due to their own negligence or malpractice. The corporate structure, however, will generally protect the professional from personal liability for corporate obligations. In a New York case, a professional corporation refused to pay for medical supplies, so the supplier sued the physician who owned the corporation. The court ruled in favor of the physician, stating that a corporation shareholder is not personally liable for the business debts of the corporation.[4]

Many people find it advantageous to use two or more corporations. For example, I have a contractor client in California who operates in California, Arizona, and Utah. I set up three specific corporations for him, one in each state, and he kept the assets of each corporation separate from the assets of the other corporations. Subsequently, his California corporation substantially underestimated costs in a major commercial development and was forced into bankruptcy. But the Arizona and Utah corporations continue to flourish in good financial health.

Lumberyards often use multiple corporations, for example, using one corporation for the wholesale and retail operation and another for the manufacturing of trusses. The truss corporation could have tremendous liability exposure if the trusses collapse in a home or commercial building, but that exposure will only affect the truss corporation and not the lumber store corporation.

Proper use of a corporate structure can greatly amplify the asset protection for professionals and other business owners, provided they comply with all state laws pertaining to incorporation and hold themselves out to the public as a corporation. But that asset protection can be lost if large amounts of real estate, cash, stocks, and other investments are placed in the corporation, since the assets of the corporation can be seized by a judgment creditor. In a well-designed system, the professional and business assets that are used by a corporation will normally be held by another corporation or by a limited partnership or trust. Refer to Chapter 22, "How Business Assets Should Be Held," which discusses how to own real estate and other business assets correctly.

Action Checklist

To avoid the risk of piercing the corporate veil:

❑ Don't commingle corporate and noncorporate money and other assets.

❑ Don't divert corporate funds or assets to personal use.

❑ Don't become personally liable for corporate debts.

❑ Document all loans to shareholders and execute formal loan agreements.

❑ Maintain corporate minutes and records.

❑ Make all transactions between related parties at arm's length.

❑ Ensure that the corporation is adequately capitalized.

❑ If you set up multiple corporations, don't maintain identical ownership or other attributes of the corporation.

Limited Partnerships Will Protect Your Assets

Rule number one: Under no circumstances should you operate your business or profession as a general partnership. Rule number two: There are no exceptions to rule number one.

Why am I so adamant on this point? It is because courts routinely hold one partner liable for the acts of the other partners. For example, four chiropractors operating as a partnership were sued jointly by a patient seen by only one of them. All four were legally responsible when the courts found the patient's doctor guilty of malpractice.

When I speak at professional meetings on this point, the reaction is stunned disbelief. Why weren't we taught this in our professional courses, I am frequently asked. I wish I knew the answer. In my opinion, structuring your professional organizations correctly to maximize protection in the event of lawsuits, litigation, or liens is the most important thing you will do in your professional life.

Professional partnerships aren't the only ones at risk. When an action for wrongful death was filed against a partner in a farm partnership, the court ruled that he could be held liable even though he did not cause the death.[1]

The liability of one partner for the acts of another comes about through interplay between two sections of the Uniform Partnership Act. One section says that the partnership is liable for any wrongful act or omission of a partner acting in the course of ordinary business. The other section holds all partners responsible for all debts and obligations of the partnership. You see how easily you can be held liable for your partner's wrongful acts even though you are innocent and unaware of his actions.

In one case, a partnership was formed by two individuals, one wealthy and one not. When the partnership defaulted on a $650,000 bank loan, the bank filed suit against the wealthy partner, ignoring the other one. The Arizona court that heard the case ruled that the creditor could sue the partnership or either partner, and was entitled to full recovery from the wealthy partner.[2]

In some states, creditors must first sue the partnership; only if partnership assets are insufficient to satisfy the judgment can the individual partners be sued. This concept offers little comfort, since most partnerships will have insufficient assets, so the partners will be sued anyway. In one Ohio case, where the partnership assets were virtually nonexistent, the court allowed the creditor to bypass suing the partnership and instead sue the individual partners directly.[3]

When two or more people go into business together, they

usually form a general partnership. A partnership is simply an association of two or more people or entities (such as a corporation) in a joint venture, business, or trade. What people may not realize is that in a general partnership, each member of the partnership is ultimately liable for the partnership's debts, and any one partner may be held liable for the entire indebtedness of the partnership. This is called "joint and several liability." Each partner may also be liable for the wrongdoing of every other member of the partnership, even if the innocent partner has no knowledge of the negligent conduct.

Here's an example. A midwestern dentist shared an office with four other dentists. They each had their own clientele, but they shared a common reception area and staff, as well as some of the accounting functions. Each dentist set his own hours, had his own practice methods, and was not accountable to the other dentists.

One of the dentists administered nitrous oxide to a child patient who experienced a severe allergic reaction and died before the medics could get him to the emergency room of the hospital. Although only one dentist was negligent, all five dentists were included in the malpractice lawsuit because they looked to the public as though they practiced together in a general partnership, when in fact there was no partnership.

One reason why so many people unwisely use a general partnership is that it is simple to form. While many partnerships have articles of partnership that clearly spell out the partnership relations, such articles aren't needed to establish a general partnership. This means that even if a partnership agreement is unwritten, a court may find that a general partnership existed—even if the persons concerned do not consider themselves to be partners.

Working with others in a general partnership can be hazardous to your financial health. In a malpractice case involving negligent treatment of a foot problem, one partner raised the defense that he had never seen the patient nor treated his foot, so he couldn't be liable. The court did not agree, and held all partners jointly and severally liable for the negligent act of only one partner.[4]

At a seminar where I was speaking I met an architect with a million-dollar problem. He had entered into a verbal partnership to buy and remodel apartments with a building contractor with whom he had worked for more than fifteen years. The contractor negotiated a million-dollar bank loan for the partnership, then took the money and ran. With his partner on the lam in Mexico, the architect was sued by the bank and held liable for the million-dollar obligation because he was in the partnership. He was forced into bankruptcy and lost everything he had spent his entire career developing. He even lost his career: Because of the incident, the state withdrew his license to practice architecture.

If you are in a general partnership, consider seriously converting your partnership into a limited partnership or a C or S corporation.

A Limited Partnership May Be the Answer

A limited partnership is a partnership having one or more limited partners, and one or more general partners. If you are the general partner, you can have complete control over all of the assets in the limited partnership, even though your ownership interest is very small.

A limited partnership differs from a general partnership in several ways, but there are four basic differences:

- The legality and formation of a limited partnership is determined by state statute. All states have enacted such statutes.
- The limited partnership must fully comply with the requirements of the statute. If it does not, it will be treated as a general partnership.
- The liability of a limited partner for partnership debts or obligations is limited to the extent of the capital he has contributed or agrees to contribute.
- The limited partners cannot share in the management or control of the limited partnership without forfeiting their limited liability.

The limited partnership is generally one of the best ways to own family assets and even business assets. A provision of the Uniform Limited Partnership Act called the "charging order" generally precludes a creditor of one of the partners from seizing assets held by the partnership. In addition, the limited partners are immunized from suits arising from an act of the limited partnership or an act of the general partner.

Using a limited partnership form of asset ownership is beneficial in three ways:

- It is a lawsuit and asset protection device.
- You can spread income among family members to lower overall family income taxes.
- It can be an advanced estate planning tool to convey interests to children during the parents' lifetimes and reducing estate taxes upon their deaths.

To create an effective limited partnership, your attorney must carefully comply with a technical requirement known as the "business purpose rule" when drafting the paperwork. The business purpose rule means that the partnership must exist for some beneficial business purpose as distinguished from a simple personal desire to be in a limited partnership. This is a fairly easy rule to comply with. If you comply with this rule, assets such as your home, bank accounts, investments, and mutual funds may be effectively transferred into one or more limited partnerships, affording you substantial asset protection.

One special type of limited partnership is the family limited partnership, which functions like other limited partnerships but is comprised of family members rather than third-party partners or investors. In a family limited partnership, you and your spouse usually act as the general partners while the children and other relatives are limited partners.

Here is an example of how a family limited partnership might be structured. You and your spouse contribute a home and some other assets to a family limited partnership. You are the general partners and retain a 5 percent ownership interest in the limited partnership. You convey a 95 percent interest in the partnership to your children or other relatives—the limited partners. From a technical standpoint, it is generally better to have each partner contribute something to the partnership even if it is only a small amount of cash or other assets. Remember, as you use this approach, you must comply with the normal gift tax rules.

If you are sued and judgment is rendered against you, here's how this family limited partnership will work to protect the assets conveyed to this type of partnership.

1. Your creditor generally gets a charging order against your limited partnership assets, but he cannot seize partnership assets (unless he is a creditor of the partnership). The charging order gives the creditor a right to the income portion of any partnership distributions, but no right to force distribution of income.
2. You, as general partner, continue to control all of the assets of the limited partnership. You may continue to draw a salary, or receive loans or other benefits, and you can pay your spouse and children management fees, investment adviser fees, and salaries for their services to the partnership.
3. The creditor cannot remove you as general partner, and has no vote or control over the affairs of the limited partnership. In general, the creditor can't unwind the partnership, nor can he force the sale of partnership assets.
4. The creditor cannot demand undistributed income from the limited partnership. If your partnership agreement was properly drafted, it will contain a clause authorizing you to retain all income for future needs of the partnership. Your creditor may now be in the unenviable position of having to pay income taxes on all the income earned by the partnership even though it is not distributed to him. The limited partnership interest will be the most worthless asset the creditor could ever hold.

It is true that a creditor may attach your small ownership interest in the partnership by way of a charging order, but this interest is so small that it is generally not worth the creditor's efforts to pursue it. Creditors will generally pursue almost any other remedy before attempting to obtain a charging order against a family limited partnership interest, because the charging order statute usually precludes attachment or levy or seizure of the assets inside the limited partnership.

When to Use a Limited Partnership

If a limited partnership is set up and recorded correctly, it will limit liability exposure. Here are some of the situations in which using a limited partnership may be appropriate:

- to control 100 percent of the family assets following a divorce
- to start over and protect your new assets from old judgments
- to hold title if both spouses are highly vulnerable to lawsuits
- to keep control of your assets even if you declare bankruptcy
- to reduce the size of your estate for estate planning purposes
- to convey assets to children without giving them control over those assets.

Individual Liability of Limited Partners

Limited partners, in general, cannot be sued individually for acts of the partnership or of the general partner, with some notable exceptions:

- if the limited partner's name is used in the firm name
- if the limited partner participates in the management of the firm

- if the limited partner's contribution to capital has not been fully received
- if the limited partner's contribution to capital has been withdrawn
- if there is a false statement in the limited partnership certificate
- if there is inadequate compliance with limited partnership statutes.

Of these exceptions, participation in management is the one that most often jettisons the asset protection of a limited partner.

The Charging Order Simplified

The charging order is the provision that provides the major remedy for a creditor of a limited partner. The laws regarding charging orders vary from state to state, but there are common elements, such as:

- The partnership may not be terminated by the creditor.
- The assets of the limited partnership may not be used to satisfy the claim of a creditor of one of the partners.
- A creditor cannot become a substituted limited partner in the partnership.
- The creditor cannot vote on matters pertaining to the partnership.
- The creditor receives the share of income from the partnership that would have gone to the debtor limited partner.

In one case, a couple transferred almost all of their real estate and stocks to a limited partnership for estate planning purposes. Two years later, a bank sued the husband for personal indebtedness, but was unable to reach the assets of the limited partnership to satisfy its claim.[5]

The longer the period of time between conveyance of assets to the partnership and the commencement of litigation, the better. If assets are transferred to a limited partnership within one year of filing for bankruptcy, it is generally considered to be a fraudulent transaction, and the assets can be taken by creditors in the bankruptcy action.

A Case Study in Applied Asset Protection

Let's look at a typical client—we'll call him Dr. Green—in need of asset protection. Dr. Green is a physician who is extremely vulnerable to litigation, and he is very concerned about his ability to continue to practice because of his increased exposure to possible lawsuits. His wife and children depend upon him for their support, but the cost of his malpractice insurance has quadrupled in the past two years. Recent judgments against other physicians in his state have exceeded the policy limits Dr. Green maintains on his liability coverage, and several malpractice insurance companies have failed in recent years.

To protect the assets of this physician, I recommend setting up four limited partnerships, as illustrated in the following charts.

Family Limited Partnership #1

I recommend transferring all liquid assets—such as cash, stocks, bonds, and mutual funds—into this limited partnership. I do not like to mix less vulnerable assets of this type with assets more vulnerable to lawsuits, such as businesses and real estate. For example, if I combined ownership of the

---

Family Limited Partnership #1
General Partners: Dr. & Mrs. Green

		Equity
Cash		$ 100,000
Stocks		250,000
Mutual funds		150,000
	Total	500,000

	Value of Interest
Dr. Green = 10% owner	$ 50,000
Mrs. Green = 90% owner	450,000

---

apartment house with his cash and investments in the same limited partnership, and an explosion in the apartment house resulted in a judgment far in excess of his policy limits, because the limited partnership owned the apartment house the judgment would allow access to all assets of the limited partnership. That would include not only the apartment house but also the cash, stocks, and other investments. The best way to minimize risk is by diversifying, transferring ownership of assets vulnerable to lawsuit into a different limited partnership from other investment assets.

Note that I have put a small percentage ownership (10 percent) in Dr. Green's name. This is in case he is sued for something unrelated to the limited partnership or his role as general partner. For example, if he crashed his plane and killed a passenger, the passenger's family could sue him as an individual. By giving Dr. Green only a small percentage ownership in the partnership, we minimize any potential recovery by a creditor of Dr. Green, since the creditor is generally limited only to a charging order as his remedy.

Family Limited Partnerships #2 and 3

I have divided the real estate ownership between two limited partnerships. (You could make a strong case for actually setting up three or four limited partnerships in this situation.) This is to prevent a creditor of one partnership from being

---

Family Limited Partnership #2
General Partner: Dr. Green

		Equity
Rental 4-plex		$ 100,000
Rental 6-plex		150,000
Commercial bldg.		150,000
	Total	400,000

		Value of Interest
Dr. Green	= 10% owner	$ 40,000
Mrs. Green	= 70% owner	280,000
Children	= 20% owners	80,000

able to reach the assets of another partnership. For example, in the event of the lawsuit resulting from the apartment house explosion mentioned above, only the assets of Partnership 3 would be vulnerable; the rental real estate and commercial building in Partnership 2 would be protected. This would not be the case were I to combine all real estate into one limited partnership.

Also note that in Limited Partnerships 2 and 3 I have added the children as limited partners. I have done this to:

- reduce the size of Dr. and Mrs. Green's estate without any effective diminution in control by Dr. Green, and to
- allow income to be allocated to the children to reduce over-all family income taxes.

Sometimes I will place as much as 90 percent of the ownership of a given limited partnership with the children and grandchildren, depending on how much estate reduction and income tax allocation is needed.

Note also that I have made Dr. Green the only general partner of Limited Partnerships 2 and 3 rather than expose Mrs. Green to the broad liabilities associated in service as a general partner. (Remember, the general partner is liable once sued on behalf of the limited partnership if the limited partnership itself is sued.) For example, let's say the general partner negligently maintains a building owned by the partnership—in fact, let's say that because of the general partner's gross negligence a fire hazard is allowed to exist in the building. If the building then catches fire and ten people are killed, the general partner, along with the limited partnership itself, can be sued. But note: The liability does not spread to

Family Limited Partnership #3	
General Partner: Dr. Green	
	Equity
20-unit apartment	$ 380,000
Vacant lot	20,000
Total	400,000
	Value of Interest
Dr. Green = 10% owner	$ 40,000
Mrs. Green = 50% owner	200,000
Children = 40% owners	160,000

the other limited partnerships—it stops the "domino" or "ripple" liability effect. In Limited Partnership 1, which owns cash and investments, liability for both the general partners and the limited partnership itself is less, and so I listed both Dr. and Mrs. Green as general partners. Also, at death, the surviving general partner automatically can become the sole successor general partner, if the limited partnership agreement so provides. In addition, this puts both spouses in an equal position of control in the event of a divorce.

Family Limited Partnership #4

Limited Partnership 4 owns assets that are extremely vulnerable to lawsuit, such as the airplane. I prefer using a limited partnership rather than a corporation because there can be adverse income tax problems to having such assets inside a corporation. (On the sale of such assets, there can be a double income tax liability if a corporation is the owner—that is, the corporation may owe taxes and the individual later may pay tax on the same income from the sale.) Also, I have made Dr. Green the only general partner of Partnership 4 because of the dangerous kinds of assets owned by this limited partnership, which are highly vulnerable to suit.

Although complex, the principles outlined in these pages are extremely important in securing the best asset protection. The biggest mistake that people make is in utilizing only one trust, limited partnership, or corporation, and transfer-

---

Family Limited Partnership #4
General Partner: Dr. Green

	Equity
Airplane	$ 150,000
Cars	20,000
Truck	10,000
Motor home	20,000
Total	200,000

	Value of Interest
Dr. Green = 30% owner	$ 60,000
Mrs. Green = 70% owner	140,000

ring all their assets to that single entity. If one asset within that entity causes a lawsuit, all assets within the entity could be lost. If you set up multiple entities, as we did for Dr. Green, each dangerous asset is protected from lawsuits against another. And by using multiple limited partnerships, you can carry that protection one step further. If your assets are in multiple limited partnerships and you are sued individually, your creditors may not seize any of the assets in the limited partnerships, but are restricted generally to a charging order. Through the charging order they can attach income available for distribution to you, but the creditor cannot seize the assets themselves. As we saw with Dr. Green, if his airplane crashed, causing injury or death, the limited partnership owning the airplane would be vulnerable to the extent of its remaining assets. If Dr. Green were found to be personally negligent, and a judgment is rendered against him personally, the courts generally rule that the assets in his other limited partnerships are not attachable or reachable by his creditor. The creditor's remedy is limited to receiving some of the income that he may be entitled to from the partnership—but not the assets.

Fraudulent Conveyances

Some people think that all they have to do is transfer an asset to their spouse, children, a trust, a corporation, or a limited partnership and they gain automatic protection. Nothing could be farther from the truth. To avoid an assertion of fraudulent conveyance, you must show that the transfer was not meant to defraud, hinder, or delay your creditors. If a creditor can show the requisite intent, then the conveyances can be set aside. This is one of the most complex areas of law and must be thoroughly understood by the attorney drafting the asset protection documents.

A transfer will be considered fraudulent if it falls into any of three categories:

- a transfer for inadequate consideration when the transferor is insolvent or the transfer will render him insolvent
- a transfer for inadequate consideration when the transferor fails to retain enough capital to meet likely future business needs
- a transfer for inadequate consideration when the transferor does not retain enough property to meet his likely future debts as they come due.

If any of the above apply, then the creditor is not required to prove the actual intent to hinder, delay, or defraud creditors. If the above do not apply, the creditor will have a difficult time proving that the conveyance was fraudulent.

The creditor generally must show that he was a creditor or about to be such at the time of the transfer. Even if that can be shown, the transferor can often overcome this burden if the same business is continued after the transfer of assets. For example, if a couple runs a lumber business as sole proprietors, and then transfer their business to a limited partnership or corporate form of doing business, this would most likely not be a fraudulent conveyance because they are continuing in the same business.[6] The couple's property (net worth) is not diminished by such a transfer because the stock takes the place of the property transferred.

This means that if you transfer your property to a limited partnership, you will probably not be found to be acting fraudulently against your creditors, especially if you remained owner of the partnership interest after the transfer. However, a transfer to a corporation or a limited partnership may be a badge of fraud if the transfer occurs and the transferor does not have the same proportional ownership in the new entity as he did originally. For example, if a husband owns 50 percent of the property that is transferred to a corporation or a limited partnership, then, to overcome the badge of fraud assertion, he must own at least 50 percent of the equity in the new entity. He might even increase his protection by owning a greater amount, such as 60 or 70 percent.

Even if a transfer can be shown to be fraudulent, the creditor must bring suit within the state statute of limitations period, which generally ranges from two to six years. If the transferor declares bankruptcy, fraudulent transfers made within one year before the filing of the bankruptcy petition can be set aside as a fraudulent conveyance.

Action Checklist

❑ If you are in a general partnership, begin immediately to consider changing your form of business operation to a corporation or limited partnership.

❑ If you are vulnerable to lawsuits—for example, a physician—consider transferring your personal assets to one or more family limited partnerships.

❑ If you own dangerous assets, such as an airplane, convey title to a limited partnership.

❑ Take these steps to avoid a finding that a transfer is an actual or a constructive fraud:
  • Don't conceal the transaction.
  • Don't make the transfer while you are being sued or threatened with suit, but if you do make the transfer upon appropriate legal advice, remember the "proportionality" principle.
  • Don't transfer substantially all of your assets.
  • Don't remove or conceal assets.
  • Don't make transfers that render you insolvent.
  • Don't make the transfer around the same time a substantial debt is incurred.

Chapter 20

Which States
Give the Best Lawsuit
Protection

What is the best state in which to incorporate? That is one of the questions I am most frequently asked, and for good reason. The state in which you incorporate makes a substantial difference in many circumstances.

If you are a professional—attorney, doctor, engineer, accountant—you must incorporate under the laws of the state in which you practice. Other businesses are not so restricted, and may incorporate in one state and do business in a different state. Why bother? Here's the reason: Your corporation internally is governed by the laws of the state in which it is incorporated, and that includes most issues relating to the rights and liabilities of officers and stockholders as well as to the internal affairs of the corporation. Incorporating in one state even though business is primarily conducted in another will result in significant lawsuit and litigation protection to of-

ficers, directors, and shareholders if the state of incorporation has more generous statutory protection provisions.

For example, if a corporation is sued in California but is incorporated in Delaware, then the California courts must generally look to the laws of the state of Delaware pertaining to
the internal affairs of the corporation, including individual liability of directors and others. On the other hand, liability for
negligent acts of the corporation itself will generally be determined by the laws of the state in which the corporation is
doing business. In the above illustration, if issues arise pertaining to liability of officers and shareholders, those issues
generally will be determined by the laws of Delaware and so
may be more favorably decided because of the more protective laws of the state of Delaware, whereas the liability of the
corporation itself will be determined by the laws of California.

The two states that have received the greatest notoriety as
defendant-protected states are Nevada and Delaware. Let's
look at the laws of those states to see why tens of thousands
of businesses have incorporated there.

The Advantage of Incorporating in Delaware

Many of the largest corporations in America are incorporated
in Delaware because the statutes of that state are drafted with
a view toward protection of corporations, officers, directors,
and shareholders in the event of litigation. Delaware statutes
provide that the stockholders of a corporation shall not be
personally liable for the corporation's debts, and also that the
corporation can eliminate the personal liability of directors
and stockholders for monetary damages for breach of duty.
The corporation may also indemnify any director, officer, em-

ployee, or agent of the corporation if he was acting in good faith in the best interests of the corporation. Few states have such provisions.

Delaware corporate law protection is often termed the "three-legged stool." The three legs of protection are:

1. limited liability of directors, so that they can be held liable only for their own personal gross negligence
2. indemnification of officers, directors, employees, and agents by the corporation itself
3. state statutes that allow the corporation to pay the premiums for directors' and officers' liability insurance.

The Advantages of Incorporating in Nevada

Nevada has laws similar to the three-legged stool approach utilized by Delaware, but in some cases, the provisions tend to be much broader with even fewer restrictions. Under Nevada law, a corporation may enact articles that reduce or eliminate personal liability for both directors and officers of the corporation, and indemnification of officers, directors, employees, and agents is mandatory. Nevada also allows the corporation to pay premiums for liability insurance on behalf of directors, officers, employees, and agents of the corporation. Nevada has further eased the burden on corporations of holding corporate meetings.

Nevada corporations have the following advantages:

- Nevada has no corporate franchise tax, corporate income tax, estate or inheritance taxes, gift taxes, or inventory taxes.
- Directors and officers can live outside Nevada.
- Shareholder names are not of public record.

- Only one director is required (hence only one person's neck is in the potential liability noose).
- Nevada is the only state that does not reciprocally exchange tax information and tax investigations with the IRS.
- Statutory liability protection for officers and directors of corporations is unsurpassed by any other state.

Most of the corporations I set up are incorporated either in the state of Delaware or the state of Nevada.

Foreign Corporation Status

A corporation is classified as domestic in the state in which it is incorporated, and it is foreign in every other state. (A corporation is alien if it is incorporated in a different country.) If you incorporate in a state other than the one in which you do business, your corporation will be considered to be a "foreign corporation" and must obtain approval to do business in your state. Every state provides for the issuance of a certificate to do business within its borders, but before a state will allow an entity incorporated in another state to do business there, it will generally require the foreign corporation to comply with certain statutory procedures. It must:

- file a copy of its charter, certificate of incorporation, or articles of association
- appoint a resident agent on whom process may be served in suits against it
- obtain a license, permit, or certificate from a designated state official
- keep designated books and records within the state and permit inspection of those records by stockholders.

A home state can, and often does, require a considerable amount of compliance by the foreign corporation before permission is granted to do business within the state. It is best to hire an attorney in the state in which you do business so he or she can file the appropriate papers with the state. Failure to comply with the procedure for registering your entity as a foreign corporation can result in substantial fines and penalties. For example, the state can fine it, deny it the privilege of using state courts, and even hold its officers, directors, or agents personally liable for corporate obligations incurred in the state.

Action Checklist

❏ Research, or ask your attorney, the requirements for incorporating in your state.

❏ Consider the protective advantages of incorporating in Delaware or Nevada. Discuss them thoroughly with your attorney. Are they sufficient for your business to outweigh the additional costs of registering in your own state as a foreign corporation?

Chapter 21

Avoiding the Dangers of Handshake Agreements

An oral agreement isn't worth the paper it's written on," Samuel Goldwyn once proclaimed. No wonder millions were shocked when actress Kim Basinger was held liable for $8.9 million for breach of an oral contract. She had orally agreed to star in a movie. When she reneged, the production company claimed it had lost millions of dollars in projected revenues and had incurred added costs. The jury agreed, and when Ms. Basinger retreated to bankruptcy court, it, too, required that she pay the award.

Even an oral agreement can be enforceable. Many business and professional people enter into oral agreements every day, and many people work together in partnerships without the benefit of a written agreement. This is a source of potential problems if one of the partners terminates association with the group. What are his or her rights to ongoing income or accounts receivable? What happens to the equipment and real estate that has been acquired? What about other assets, such as library or patient lists? And what obligation does he or she have to the partnership for future lawsuits and losses that had their genesis while the partner was associated with the group? Oral partnerships are fraught with dangers: Never consider an association with anyone unless that association is spelled out in a comprehensive written agreement.

An oral association is generally considered to be a general partnership, and brings with it awesome liability exposure for each member of the association, even for the acts of the other associates. Earlier in this book I related the story of a group of dentists sharing office space who were held liable for the death of a young patient from an allergic reaction to nitrous oxide. Those dentists were held by the courts to be operating in an "oral" partnership. Had they instead associated in a written corporation, they could have had limited liability to the doctor who committed the malpractice rather than each becoming jointly and severally liable for the negligent act.

The General Rule of Law

Courts have held oral contracts to be completely binding, even if they are of a personal nature. For example, a fifty-year-old rancher in Montana broke off his engagement to a woman from the Midwest. Although he told her to keep the $10,000 engagement ring and gave her another $10,000 in cash, she sued him for breach of promise to marry. The jury found him liable for an additional $100,000 in damages for his breach of the oral promise to marry. While this kind of case is rare, it illustrates the potential dangers of oral agreements.

Agreements can be partly written and partly oral, particularly if all of the details are not covered in a written contract. One of the parties may assert that there were additional oral understandings between the parties that were not included in the written agreement. The courts generally hold that if the written agreement appears to be complete and is clearly intended to express the full and complete agreement and intentions of the parties, oral evidence will not be allowed to be introduced.

If the terms of the agreement are plain and unambiguous, the court will not allow the introduction of oral evidence. However, a written agreement may be made and later modified orally. The law recognizes that written contracts may be modified by a subsequent contract, and that contract may be expressed as written, oral, or implied. If it appears that the parties were acting in contravention to their agreement, it is likely that the courts would find that the agreement had been modified.

The Unwritten Association

Unwritten associations abound in America. Remember that if you are in an oral joint venture, whether it is real estate investing, landscaping, the practice of law or medicine, or even operating a retail outlet, the law is very explicit. Even though you have no written agreement, you are nonetheless in general partnership and all partners and associates may be held jointly and severally liable for the act of one of the other members. All partners are liable for wrongdoing of one of the partners acting within the scope of the business, although they do not participate in or have knowledge of the negligent conduct.

Dangers of the Oral Contract

Too many people today try to sell businesses under either an oral contract or a skimpily written sales document. For example, two parties corresponded about a sales deal, and one party agreed to buy the assets of the other party's business. No written contract was drawn up, and when the purchaser reneged, the courts found that the oral contract was unenforceable and there were not sufficient writings, even though there had been mention in their letters, to constitute a valid written contract.[1]

In another case, the parties reached a detailed oral agreement regarding the purchase price, payments to be made, the interest rate to be paid, and the length of the buyout. When disputes later arose between the parties, the court held that the oral contract was simply not enforceable, and reminded the parties that sales contracts should be in writing.[2]

This seems elementary, but it is all too common. Oral contracts may have been sufficient in the good old days, but they are clearly perilous in today's marketplace.

Action Checklist

Here is my advice on the subject of unwritten agreements and unwritten associations:

❑ Never enter into an oral, unwritten agreement. All agreements, no matter how simple, should be in writing.

❑ All associations with others in any kind of a business or an investment activity must be in writing. Never enter into a business or professional association with anyone else unless the terms of the undertaking have been reduced to writing. Oral agreements have been a very fruitful and extensive source of litigation, and will remain so as long as people ignore this basic advice.

Chapter 22

How Business Assets Should Be Held

I met an old friend on the street who knew I did a lot of asset protection and estate planning work. He told me of a friend of his who had developed a successful new specialty, suing business owners. To my surprise, when I asked whether he practiced any other kind of law, he told me he wasn't a lawyer at all. He was a former business owner who found he could make more money suing others than he ever had as a businessman. In just two years he was awarded five homes and commercial buildings and he was about to seize a sixth.

Many people have become adept at suing. These "professional plaintiffs" often commence lawsuits with only a slim chance of winning; however, they know that defendants will often cut a deal and settle a lawsuit quickly rather than devote the time and expense it will take to go to trial. These professional plaintiffs will target business owners with plenty to lose, and a judgment against a business can result in the loss of the business real estate. Similarly, non–real estate investments can also be lost to a judgment creditor. Insurance may not protect you if the insurance policy contains exclusionary clauses or if the amount of liability protection is inadequate.

The Plan

Years ago, armed with an MBA and contemplating law school, I taught some undergraduate university courses in finance, tax, and business. I must confess that I taught those students that there was no reason for the complexity of multiple corporations: One corporation would do the trick, even if it operated many different businesses. Today, I wish I could contact every one of those students and confess I was wrong. If you want to protect yourself in today's litigious society, you must learn to design multiple entities to ensure your financial survival. You must always anticipate that litigation, liens, wrongful termination actions, seizures, levies, and EPA actions can destroy you financially.

Review carefully the nature of your business and professional activities. Can you logically divide that business or professional activity into two or more separate entities? The more the better. Divvying up ownership of your assets may confuse your banker, but it can definitely save your assets.

Real Estate Used in Your Business

Business real estate generally should be owned by an entity other than the business. In most situations, you can gain substantial asset protection by separating the real estate ownership from the entity that is using the real estate. If owning and leasing real estate is your business, the real estate should then be owned by other entities, such as limited partnerships or trusts; the business operation itself should be a separate, distinct legal entity, such as a corporation.

I have a client who owns three apartment buildings, and we have placed the buildings into three separate limited partnerships. If one limited partnership is sued because of faulty wiring in the apartment building it owns, the other limited partnerships and their assets will be protected. Sometimes, additional protection is provided by structuring the ownership in this way, then leasing the buildings to an operating corporation to manage them. Many attorneys believe this provides enhanced protection.

In our law firm, we generally recommend to clients that real estate used by a business be owned by a separate legal entity and leased to the business. For example, we recommended to a group of eight Dallas doctors that they transfer title to their building into a limited partnership owned by the eight doctors and their families. The limited partnership then leased the building to the physicians' medical practice, which was incorporated. In the event of a malpractice suit against the doctors, the real estate owned in this manner was now generally immune from loss. Had the doctors done nothing, a malpractice lawsuit could have resulted in loss of the entire medical complex. Most business owners in this country are vulnerable to this kind of loss. They spend much more time on accumulating wealth than on protecting that wealth.

The written lease between the entities is critical. We generally advise our clients to structure the lease so that all liability flows to the tenant. That means your business or professional corporation has the responsibility to maintain the premises, provide upkeep and repairs, insure the property, and defend in the case of a lawsuit. I make the tenant fully responsible for all defects, and the tenant agrees to be solely responsible for making the real estate safe and usable by all who come on the premises. Here's why:

A woman who had tripped and fractured her hip was awarded $600,000 in a suit against the people associated with the office building where she was injured. The court then had to decide who should be required to pay those damages. The owner of the building was absolved of responsibility because the property had been leased under a tightly drawn agreement that made the lessee responsible for the maintenance of the property, and also provided that in the event of any legal action, the lessee would have to indemnify the owner.[1]

In a similar case in Louisiana, the owner of the real estate used by a fishing camp was not liable when someone fell through some steps and was injured. The lease held the owner harmless for any hazard of which he had not been notified, and the tenant had assumed the responsibility for maintenance and upkeep. The lease further provided for indemnification to the owner.[2]

Generally, a lease is one of two types. One contains clauses designed to protect the owner (lessor) of the real estate, while the other is designed to protect the tenant (lessee) by transferring many of the responsibilities back to the owner. It is dangerous to simply use a lease form that you purchase at an office-supply store. It is well worth your time and expense to have a lease agreement drafted that protects you if you are the real estate owner, or, in the alternative, protects you if you are the tenant.

What happens if both the lessor and the lessee read this

book? In all likelihood, the lease they sign will not favor either the lessor or the lessee. Rather, they and their attorneys will negotiate each major issue, and will draft a lease that reflects their negotiated agreement. For example, the lease might provide that the property taxes will be paid by the owner of the property, but that the tenant will maintain the insurance and must provide a copy of the insurance policy to the owner. Some lease forms provide a list of key issues, such as property taxes, insurance, window breakage, wiring and painting, major maintenance, and minor maintenance. Space is provided where the signers can check whether it is the tenant or the owner who will be responsible for each type of expense.

My general approach with clients is that real estate used in a business should be held in a limited partnership because of the advanced lawsuit protection afforded by these entities. Another option is titling the real estate in the name of a separate corporation, but this may create major tax problems. Real estate could also be placed into the living trust of the less vulnerable spouse, or given to the children or conveyed to a children's trust for their benefit. This last arrangement has the additional advantage of allowing the rents and lease income from the real estate to go to the children, often reducing the overall income taxes of the family.

Potential Environmental Disasters with Your Real Estate

Laws concerning environmental hazards add a whole new area of potential liability to owning real estate.

I was teaching a seminar in Florida when a man approached me. "Jay," he said, "I have a piece of property down-

town appraised for $8 million that has a $1 million bank loan
on it. I'd be glad to give it to you for free." It turns out that a
former owner had dumped toxic chemicals in the back of the
property and it had contaminated the soil. There is now a potential $12 million EPA fine, and under federal EPA laws, the
present owner of the property is liable for the fine even
though it was a previous owner who dumped the chemicals.
The bank even refused to foreclose on its $1 million mort-
gage because, as the new owner, it could become liable for
the $12 million fine.

A man who left a job with a large corporation to go into business for himself bought an old gas station in Magna, Utah, to
use as an auto mechanic shop. He didn't realize that there
were three old two-thousand-gallon gasoline tanks buried be-
neath the land. Those tanks had leaked, and federal law requires him, as owner of the property, to clean up any toxic
wastes. The cost of cleaning up the property will be far more
than his original purchase price of $40,000, and he faces ad-
ditional state and federal fines. Had he purchased the property in the name of a corporation, limited liability company,
or a limited partnership, the likelihood is that he could have
avoided personal fines and the probable bankruptcy he now
faces.

What could these men have done differently? The general
rule I follow is to acquire property in the name of a corporation, a limited partnership, or a limited liability company that
will provide substantial protection in the event of just such
problems. I will never acquire any real estate in my name, my
wife's name, or joint ownership or in my wife's trust or my living trust. Never! I always acquire properties in the name of
an entity that will protect me and my family from loss.

How Other Business Assets Should Be Held

More than 90 percent of businesses I examine are wrongly structured initially. Imagine, then, my surprise when I found that my new clients, four brothers who owned a hotel, had structured their hotel business correctly. They came to me because they were being sued, and they were very matter-of-fact about it. "We knew that the hotel business is dangerous and that this would happen one day," remarked one of the brothers. "That is why we decided to set up our hotel operation this way."

The four brothers set up a corporation to operate and manage the hotel and employees. That corporation held few valuable assets. The hotel building and land were put into a limited partnership, the ownership of which was divided between the four families. The limited partnership then leased the hotel building and land to the corporation.

I congratulated the brothers for seeking out advisers who would suggest advanced planning to guard against future lawsuits. "Oh, no," said one brother. "We did a lot of reading and studying on our own and decided ourselves how we should set up the hotel operation. When we told our advisers what we wanted done, they opposed it. They said Americans generally don't structure businesses this way. But we said, 'Do it anyway.' "

And thank goodness they had. Although the lawsuit, plus other financial problems, put the corporation on the verge of bankruptcy, the valuable hotel building and land were insulated and protected.

We generally set up hotel operations so that the land and building are owned by a limited partnership but the hotel operation itself is run by a separate corporation. The limited partnership leases the land and building to the operating corporation. The hotel business is a potentially dangerous business. If someone is injured or killed or an employee files a wrongful termination lawsuit, judgment would usually be rendered against the hotel corporation. The operating corporation could go bankrupt without affecting the limited partnership that owns the hotel building and land.

In 1992, the Marriott Corporation divided their operations into two corporations. The Marriott International Corporation would own trade names, reservation and franchise systems, and its business would be operating the hotels and service businesses. The Host Marriott Corporation, as successor to the existing company, would own the hotel properties and other assets, and assumed the Marriott's $2.9 billion of debt. This was a positive move toward modern asset protection, using multiple entities instead of one, and separating the operating entity, which is the most likely to be sued, from the less vulnerable asset-owning entity. I wondered what took them so long to implement this concept. They could have learned a thing or two many years ago from the four brothers who owned just one hotel.

Protect One Business When Another Is Sued

Two businesses should never operate together without legal separation of the entities. In fact, even if you operate only one business, you should separate the components of that business to protect yourself if you are sued. At a recent meeting of the Chicago Dental Convention I encouraged dentists to use one professional corporation for the practice of dentistry and a separate and distinct corporation for a dental laboratory with which they may be involved.

A lumber store I advised is also structured for effective asset protection. The lumber store real estate, including the land and building, is owned by a family limited partnership. The lumber store itself is operated by a corporation. The manufacture of trusses is conducted by another separate corporation. Why all this effort? The lumber store could be a defendant in a wrongful termination action or perhaps be sued because a defective can of paint blew up or even because a twenty-five-cent gumball caused illness. We did not want a lawsuit against the lumber store to close down the truss manufacturing business. Nor did we want a lawsuit against the lumber store to result in seizure of the land and building. Most importantly, because of the danger of truss manufacturing, we did not want a judgment against the truss business to deplete the lumber store or result in seizure of the land and the buildings.

One ski resort with six ski runs has set up a separate corporation for each ski run. One group in New York City has over twenty corporations. Each corporation owns two taxicabs.

An Example

Here is how I would work with a typical client. Mr. Jones owns three businesses, consisting of a car wash, an income tax service, and a home remodeling business. In addition, he owns the car wash building and a separate building for the tax service. I would set up three separate C corporations to run each of the businesses. I would then create two limited partnerships, each of which would own one building. I would create one lease between the car wash corporation and the limited partnership that owns the car wash building. Then I would execute a second lease between the income tax service corporation and the limited partnership that owns the building where the tax service is located. (Under certain circumstances, I might use trusts or even limited liability companies in lieu of limited partnerships.)

The profits of each operating business will probably be paid as salary to the owner who operates the business. Two of the operating corporations will also make lease payments to the limited partnership that owns the building in which it is housed. This offers a significant income tax advantage to a family wanting to pass income to children to be taxed at their lower tax rates. (Remember, though, that children younger than fourteen are taxed at their parents' tax rates.) For example, if Mr. Jones has teenage children, he can make them the primary limited partners, and the lease income will be taxed to them. The money could be accumulated for their college educations or other special needs. A one-year lease allows for a greater deductible lease payment than does a three-year lease, which must have a lower annual lease payment. So if the needs of the children are high, Mr. Jones will want to use the shorter lease period for the leases. Even if the partners are not the children, for superior asset protection Mr. Jones may wish to utilize shorter lease terms in order to maximize the transfer of funds from the operating corporations to the limited partnerships, because the limited partnership has superior lawsuit protection for cash and other assets it accumulates than does the corporation.

Although many entities are involved, the basic principle of

asset protection is simple: Separate the operations that are vulnerable to lawsuit from the assets to be protected. Many professionals expect the day will come when accountants, attorneys, and financial planners will be vulnerable to lawsuits themselves—for poor advice—each time they recommend the traditional approach of setting up one corporation to operate the business and hold all assets rather than structuring businesses with multiple entities for maximum protection.

An Analysis of the Law

The courts will generally consider two corporations you set up as separate and distinct, and will agree that one is not merely the alter ego of the other, if all corporate formalities are maintained independently for the two separate entities. The mere fact that corporations share the same officers and directors, or even the same owners, will not automatically destroy the separateness of the corporations, or cause the courts to pierce the corporate veil.

Complete disregard of corporate formalities for your multiple corporations will, however, cause multiple problems. The corporate veil will be pierced where a corporation is created or used for an improper purpose, or where the corporate form has been abused. Many factors are considered, including whether the corporation formalities have been disregarded, whether the corporation was undercapitalized, whether there has been intermingling of corporate and personal funds, whether there has been payment of corporate dividends, whether there has been siphoning of funds by the stockholders, and whether the debtor corporation was insolvent at the time. The courts may also consider whether the same office or business locations were used by the corporation and its individual stockholders, whether there was an absence of corporate records, whether there are nonfunctioning officers or directors, whether there was a diversion of the corporation's funds or assets to noncorporate uses, whether there was failure to maintain an arm's length relationship, and whether there is such domination and control of the corporation that it is indistinguishable from the shareholder.

If two or more corporations or other entities are used, each must comply precisely with state laws. State and federal tax returns should be filed, meetings should be held, and advertising and promotion should be done in the name of each separate entity. Ask your attorney to help you design a checklist of the procedures that you must follow to maintain the separateness and independence of the two legal business entities. Remember that a corporation requires much more stringent compliance than a limited partnership does—for example, a limited partnership has no requirement for monthly, quarterly, or annual meetings.

In a case involving breach of contract, two corporations were sued even though the contract was with just one. Testimony revealed that the two corporations were very closely tied together, and that correspondence for both corporations was sent to just one of the corporations. The court found that because the corporations were so intimately linked, they were in essence acting as one contracting entity, and that the corporations' affairs were indistinguishable one from the other. In the words of the court, if there is evidence of "blending of identities, or a blurring of lines of distinction, both formal and substantive, between two corporations or between an individual and a corporation, factors such as identity of shareholders, directors, officers and employees, failure to distinguish in ordinary business between the two entities, and failure to observe proper formalities, are important." The separateness of the two entities disappears; therefore each corporation is liable for the acts of the other.[3]

It is important to set up your business structure carefully, but as the above case shows, it is equally important to adhere to the letter of the law.

In a similar case, an insolvent corporation was sued by someone who leased property from it. Because the corporation was insolvent, the plaintiff also sued a related corporation that had deeper pockets, arguing that the corporations weren't really separate entities and should be joined together in the suit as one entity. The court disagreed. In order for the second corporation to be liable for the first corporation's debts, it reasoned, the plaintiff must establish that "the corporation was so controlled and manipulated that it had become a mere instrumentality of another." The plaintiff was unable to prove that the two corporations were not separate, and that recognizing two separate entities would sanction fraud or promote injustice.[4]

To determine whether two corporations are really separate and distinct with neither accountable for the acts of the other, the courts generally look for:

- a lack of attention to corporate formalities
- assets of the two corporations that are commingled
- operations that are intertwined
- evidence of complete domination and control by one corporation over the other.[5]

In another interesting case, a large conglomerate of family real estate businesses and multiple corporations was sued.

The court found that the lines of control and responsibility were blurred among the many family businesses and inter-related corporations. For example, the various corporations had the same office, office staff, and the same directors and officers. The court also found a great deal of financial inter-mingling. Funds were shifted from one account to another, and the corporations did not deal at arm's length with each other. The court ruled that the corporations weren't really separate and distinct, but rather acted together in unison as one entity and that each entity was therefore responsible for the debts of the others.[6]

In another case involving a personal injury action, the em-ployee sued the corporation for which he worked and also the parent corporation. Although the parent corporation was in-volved in the day-to-day activities and operation of the sub-sidiary corporation, the court concluded that the parent did not dominate and control the subsidiary. The court observed that the two corporations maintained separate books, records, bank accounts, offices, and staff, and that each con-sulted its own financial advisers, accountants, and stockbro-kers. The court refused to pierce the corporate veil and hold the parent company liable for the judgment against the sub-sidiary corporation.[7]

The Dangers of Owning and Using Business Assets Incorrectly

It is best to structure your business and assets correctly from the beginning, but if you have not, it is not too late to do so. As a matter of fact, I remember one couple who came to see me after they had unwittingly gotten into trouble with the U.S. government as well as with two states, and they were facing multiple legal actions. Although it appeared that they were coming to me too late, we carefully transferred their assets into limited partnerships. We knew that the transfers could possibly be found in violation of fraudulent conveyance laws, and thus unwound, but it would have been tragic in their innocent situation not to at least try to protect these assets. I wasn't paid for my services, and ended up writing off the bill. But eight years later, the couple appeared, checkbook in hand. "We've come to pay your bill," the husband said. "We are grateful for what you did, and are now in a position to pay you. Everything you did worked, and our house and other assets were saved by using the limited partnership."

Once a business finds itself in financial difficulties, it is generally too late to protect its assets. An insolvent business cannot dispose of its assets without receiving proper consideration and deprive its creditors of the collection of their debts. In general, if a creditor is awarded a judgment against a debtor, the creditor may go to the debtor's place of business with a sheriff armed with a levy and seize the assets.

It is tempting for the business owner to try to get rid of the corporate assets before they can be seized, but consider the following case. A corporation agreed to remodel a home, and then walked off the site when a conflict arose. The homeowner sued and was awarded over $60,000 in damages against the corporation. Meanwhile, the owner of the corporation depleted all of the assets of the corporation so that the homeowner wouldn't be able to get anything. The court ruled that the corporation's owner was personally liable because he had wasted the assets of the corporation, and so the homeowner was able to collect from him personally. It is fairly routine in law that if a corporation's owner, director, or officer wastes or depletes the business assets, then the officers, directors, and even the shareholders can become personally liable.[8]

Although I advocate using multiple entities for asset protection, I don't advocate doing it in an attempt to hide assets. In one case a corporation, to avoid a creditor, transferred all of its assets into a second corporation, which in turn transferred all of its assets to a third corporation. This series of maneuvers both looked and smelled like fraud, and the court disregarded all the transfers and allowed the judgment creditor to reach the assets regardless of their having been transferred to other entities.[9]

Sometimes a failing corporation will sell company assets to family and friends for a minimal amount of money to evade a potential corporate creditor. In one case, property worth $25,000 was sold for $25. The court held that the transfer was fraudulent and was an obvious attempt to get rid of the assets and make them unreachable by the corporation's creditor. The creditor was allowed to seize the assets anyway.[10]

In another case, assets were transferred from a subsidiary corporation to its parent corporation to evade a judgment creditor. The court held that the creditor could seize assets from both the subsidiary corporation and its parent corporation.[11]

Bankruptcy

When setting up a new business, you must anticipate and plan for what will happen if your business fails. The bankruptcy code says that the bankruptcy trustee may seize all of the debtor's nonexempt property, even if it is necessary to carry on the business. A corporation may be forced into bankruptcy, either voluntarily or involuntarily, and all of the assets of the corporation, including real estate, equipment, inventory, and accounts receivable may now be controlled by the trustee in bankruptcy. Begin with that in mind when you structure your business, and structure your business entities for maximum asset protection.

Now that you know the risks and advantages of using multiple entities, you must decide which structure is best for your businesses. Devise a checklist to help you pinpoint the compliance that is necessary to adhere to the rules and regulations governing those entities. Keep the entities as separate as possible. Your financial survivability in today's world depends on it.

Action Checklist

❏ If you are setting up a new business, use different entities, whether corporations or partnerships, to insulate valuable assets from operations that are likely to be sued.

❏ If your business is already ongoing, it isn't too late. Go to an expert in asset protection to discuss ways to transfer assets from existing corporations to a more protected structure. There are two good ways to do this:

  • Sell the assets to another entity from the corporation at a low, but honest, fair market value, or
  • Distribute corporate assets as tax-deductible salary and wages to corporate officers.

Action Checklist (continued)

❑ Make a list of all the real estate you presently own and how it is titled.

❑ Consider transferring real estate used by your business into a limited partnership or a limited liability company, or into your spouse's living trust or a children's trust.

❑ Decide which entity would best hold the real estate, and meet with your attorney to create the entity and transfer the real estate.

❑ Have a lease agreement drafted between your business and that entity, and scrupulously comply with all provisions of that lease agreement.

Chapter 23

How to Protect Against Customer Lawsuits

Insurance can save your business from financial disaster, but exclusionary clauses sometimes render your insurance worthless. At a seminar recently I met a university professor who had invested in a small rental house. His tenant's grandson had come to visit and had ingested lead-based paint from nibbling on walls and doorjambs. The family filed a $5 million lawsuit for the child's permanent injuries, and the insurance company refused coverage because of a lead-base-paint exclusion in the policy. The professor was afraid of losing all the assets he had accumulated over his lifetime because of this tragic accident.

Even if the mishap isn't excluded from coverage, damage awards often exceed policy limits. In Maryland, a patient won a $2.5 million lawsuit against her anesthesiologist for malpractice. The doctor carried only $1 million of malpractice insurance, so the patient sued the doctor individually for the difference between the malpractice insurance and the amount of the judgment.[1]

On a cross-country flight, I struck up a conversation with another attorney who happened to be seated next to me. He told me he specialized in suing attorneys and physicians for malpractice. Since our law firm specializes in protecting clients from lawsuits, we had a lively conversation. One of the most interesting things he told me was that his law firm primarily pursued those professionals who had liability insurance or assets that were sizable and could be seized. He said his motivation to sue disappeared if there was little insurance and if the professional's assets had been protected and placed beyond the reach of creditors.

Now I am not suggesting that you drop all liability insurance. I believe in the value of liability and malpractice insurance. On the other hand, it is interesting to understand what motivates many attorneys to file lawsuits on behalf of their clients. The bottom line is, you must carry liability insurance, but you must also protect your assets, or a business or professional judgment against you could allow the creditor to seize not only your business assets but your personal assets as well.

How to Protect Business and Professional Assets

People often fail to protect their assets out of ignorance or laziness. Are you willing to lose everything in the event of a lawsuit? If not, consider structuring your business like this:

- First, use a corporation to conduct your business or professional activities.

- Second, separate out the real estate, equipment, and other major assets from the business itself and convey them to a separate corporation, trust, or limited partnership. These assets can then be leased to the corporation, and are thus generally insulated from seizure by corporate creditors.

One popular approach is to place business assets such as real estate into a limited partnership owned by the spouse or children. In the event of judgment against both the business and the business owner, these assets are generally protected and not subject to seizure, levy, or attachment by the business creditor.

I had a husband and wife in my office who lost their clothing store, and ultimately their home, because of tax problems and two lawsuits. It sickens me that people suffer because they failed to implement even the most elementary asset protection. I empathize with creditors who are damaged and I believe that business owners and professionals have an obligation to those with whom they deal. But this ethical obligation can be met by having adequate insurance that is available to an injured client, patient, or customer. If you do not protect your assets through proper business structuring, punitive damages and excessive judgment awards can destroy your family, leading even to suicide, addiction, or family breakup.

Protecting Your Assets If Your Partner or Associate Is Sued

The risks are very high that a patient or customer may sue you for negligent acts of your partner or associate. If your business is incorrectly structured, you may be held individually liable for those acts even though you did nothing wrong. As a business owner, your most critical decision is the selection of the type of legal entity under which you will do business.

A corporation generally insulates officers, directors, and shareholders from the acts or obligations of the corporation if they are not participants in wrongful conduct, and also protects these people from the negligent act of another corporate officer, director, or shareholder. I therefore recommend that most businesses and professionals establish a corporation as their initial line of defense. Remember that general partnerships and proprietorships provide little protection for your individual assets in the event of litigation. Remember also that if you place valuable assets in your corporation, those assets can be lost to creditors in the event of a judgment against the corporation.

A professional accountancy corporation signed an employment contract with a new accountant. When the accountant later sued for wrongful termination, the court found the individual shareholder accountants not liable, because the employment contract was properly structured and entered into by the corporation itself.[2]

The Role of Insurance

It is critical that you have liability insurance sufficient to protect you in the event of a lawsuit. A California court recently rendered a $1.5 million award to the parents of a child injured in a swimming pool at an apartment complex where the child lived. The owner of the apartment complex, who carried only $300,000 in liability insurance, then sued the insurance company for failing to counsel him to carry the proper amount of insurance. The court gave his unique argument no credence, leaving the apartment owner facing a judgment well in excess of his insurance coverage.[3]

If all business owners would select the proper form of doing business, generally a corporation, and maintain adequate liability insurance, most of the grief and loss suffered by business owners and professionals would be eliminated.

Action Checklist

❑ If your business is not currently incorporated, consider doing so immediately.

❑ Separate out the real estate, equipment, and other major assets from the business itself and convey them to a separate corporation, trust, or limited partnership.

❑ Obtain liability insurance sufficient to protect both your business and you individually in the event of a lawsuit.

Chapter 24

How to Protect Against Lawsuits Involving Employees

As an employer, you are vulnerable to several types of lawsuits involving employees, the most common of which are lawsuits for employee negligence, lawsuits for employee sexual harassment, and wrongful termination suits.

Employee Negligence

Countless employers are sued each year for the negligent acts of their employees. Here are two examples from my files:

Case #1. The owner of a small automobile body shop sent an employee on an errand in a company car. The employee ran a stop sign and killed the father of three young children. Result: The employer was sued, and ultimately declared bankruptcy.

Case #2. An employee on an errand in a company car left the car parked illegally on the side of the road. A Las

Vegas couple slammed into the parked vehicle, killing the driver. The unprotected business owner was named in a multimillion-dollar lawsuit.

In general, an employer is liable for the negligent act of an employee committed within the course of business activities. This is true even if the employee is off duty, as long as the employee is on a business errand. For example, a waitress ran an errand for her restaurant after her shift. She was involved in an accident that seriously injured a pedestrian. The court held that even though the waitress's shift had ended, she was still acting within the scope of her employment and the restaurant was liable for the accident.[1] For this reason, whenever possible, have supplies delivered to you by the supplier himself rather than asking an employee to run an errand or pick up supplies.

As an employer, you may even be held liable for acts you forbade your employee to commit. The U.S. Supreme Court allowed an accident victim to sue a ski resort when its employee collided with another skier, even though the employer had told the employee not to jump off that particular crest because it was too dangerous.[2]

An employer may, however, have some protection from the illegal acts of his employee. An employee on his way to deliver payroll checks to a work site decided to get high on cocaine. An accident resulted, and the court held that the driver had deviated from his duties and wasn't acting within the scope of his employment when he consumed the cocaine. Therefore the employer was not held liable for injuries sustained in the accident.[3]

To minimize their liability exposure, many employers have restructured their businesses so that they hire independent contractors rather than employees for certain business activities. Although this approach has worked quite effectively in many circumstances, sometimes it may not. For example, if a bricklayer negligently drops a brick from a scaffolding and it strikes a pedestrian, the contractor who hired the bricklayer may be liable for any damages, even if the bricklayer was an independent contractor rather than an employee.

A far more effective approach is for the employer to structure his business correctly. For example, the business could act as a corporation, with all employees working for that specific corporation. Most of the assets would be kept out of the corporation, in a second corporation or a trust or limited partnership, and would be leased to the corporation. Proper structuring of the business itself can go a long way toward protection of employers from acts of employees.

Protection for the Employee

If you are an employee, there are steps you can take to protect yourself from lawsuits. An employee can be held liable for his own negligent acts even though he was acting in his capacity of employee at the time. The employee may be protected from liability, however, if he has a bona fide indemnification agreement with his employer, which says that the employer will reimburse him for any damages he sustains as the result of a lawsuit for his actions as an employee. In a Minnesota case, an ambulance was involved in an accident while transporting a patient to the hospital, and the patient was paralyzed as a result. Both the driver and his employer were held to be liable for damages.[4] Had the employee obtained indemnification from the employer, he would have had a right of reimbursement for any losses he sustained as a result of the lawsuit.

Many lawsuits against businesses arise from injuries to employees and others caused by equipment malfunction. When an employee in a fast-food restaurant was injured by malfunctioning equipment, the employer was held liable, even though he was personally unaware of the danger of the equipment.[5] In another case, malfunctioning equipment caused a flood, and the employee of a company hired to clean up the mess slipped and fell. The owner of the equipment was liable for a $350,000 judgment against him.[6]

Generally, both the employer and the employee will be held liable for the negligent act of an employee. Many employment contracts are lopsided in favor of the employer unless the employee has his own attorney review the proposed contract. Sometimes the employee will negotiate an employment contract that provides that the employee will be indemnified by the employer for any negligence. This clause could be modified to provide that the employee will be indemnified by the employer for negligent acts, but not if the act is willful, deliberate, or reckless.

Wrongful Termination Suits

The first step toward protection against wrongful termination suits is to correctly structure your business so that any judgment will go against the corporation rather than you personally. Never do business as a proprietorship. Not only do you risk your own assets, but you also run the risk that the courts will hold that a proprietorship is nothing more than an oral general partnership that includes your spouse and sometimes even your children. This greatly increases a plaintiff's pool of lawsuit victims from which to seize assets.

How Pervasive Are Wrongful Termination Suits?

A survey conducted by the law firm of Jackson, Lewis, Schnitzler and Krupman polled 1,014 industrial relations executives at Fortune 500 companies in Atlanta, Boston, Los Angeles, New York City, and the New York metropolitan area. Half of the survey respondents said their companies had been hit with wrongful discharge suits during the past year. Patrick Vaccaro, managing partner of the law firm, was shocked at what they found. "We've known for a long time that litigation in this area had increased, but this finding was surprising. It's a very large percentage. The workforce these days is much more aware of individual rights. They are more aggressive and less loyal to the company."

Your probability of being hit with an employee lawsuit is high. It is imperative that you structure your business and manage it with this likelihood in mind.

The Legal Basis for Wrongful Termination Suits

The second part of protecting yourself is to understand the law concerning wrongful termination. The "master and servant" relationship controls the ability of a terminated employee to file suit against an employer. By virtue of this relationship, an employee may hold an employer liable for breach of an employment contract, whether written or oral. A wrongful discharge is tantamount to a breach of the employment contract. An employee owes a fiduciary duty to his employer to serve the employer honestly, faithfully, and loyally. The employee must act for the employer's benefit and not injure the business of the employer or compete with him. If the employee fails to act accordingly, the employer may discharge him. However, an employer has no right to discharge an employee if he is motivated by a specific intent to harm the employee or to act in bad faith. For example, an employer may not fire an employee simply because he dislikes the employee.

The employer may, of course, fire an employee for cause, but it must be good cause. In one case, an employee was fired for two improprieties during a six-year employment: making a thirteen-cent personal phone call and taking a day off work to attend an undocumented physical therapy session. The employee sued for wrongful discharge and was awarded over $13 million.[7]

Employee Handbooks and Contracts

An employee handbook can protect you from both negligence claims and wrongful termination suits by clearly spelling out your employees' responsibilities. The employee handbook represents advance notice to employees of the employer's expectations. If you terminate someone for documented violation of those rules and regulations, your action will likely be found to be for cause rather than in bad faith.

The rules contained in an employee handbook must be reasonable. One employee handbook contained a disclaimer that stated the employer could terminate any employee without notice. This is called an "at-will" type of employment. When the employer was sued by a worker who had been terminated for calling in sick, the U.S. Supreme Court held that the handbook provisions were insufficient to constitute at-will employment and the employee was awarded damages.[8]

Similarly, an explicit employment contract can serve to show cause for termination if the employee does not fulfill its terms. However, you must be careful not to draft conditions in the handbook that could be construed to be breaches of the employment agreement. In one case an employee was hired under a written agreement. Later, a handbook was issued to all employees, and the employee was subsequently fired for violation of the rules in the handbook. But the handbook rules were in conflict with the employment contract, and the employee was awarded $130,000 for wrongful termination.[9]

Will Insurance Cover?

Most employers believe their liability insurance coverage will protect them from all forms of litigation. Check your insurance carefully: Wrongful termination lawsuits may not be covered. An employer who settled a sexual harassment and wrongful termination lawsuit for $1 million found that his insurance policy contained an exclusionary provision, which stipulated that the insurance company was not liable to cover an employer's intentional acts. Because wrongful termination of an employee is generally defined as an intentional act of an employer, there was no coverage in this case. The employer was totally responsible for the $1 million award, without any resort to his company insurance.[10]

If you have employees, in anticipation of your potential liability for employee negligence you should purchase as broad a liability policy for your business as possible. One corporation with the foresight to purchase broad liability insurance protection, including officer's and director's liability insurance, was extremely grateful for it when socked with an $11 million lawsuit from an employee who claimed he was wrongfully terminated.[11]

Rightful Termination of an Employee

As an employer, you have the right to terminate an employee for good cause. So it is important to establish "good cause" that will support a termination. You should have periodic (annual or semiannual) job performance evaluation interviews with each employee, circulate periodic personnel memos explaining policies and procedures, and conduct periodic staff meetings with minutes maintained of those meetings. Whenever you encounter an action that could justify a potential termination, you should immediately have a face-to-face meeting with the employee, in what is often called a warning interview. In such interviews, the company should document in writing the substance of the accusation and the general nature of the meeting and the reaction of both the employee and the employer. Insert this written document into the employee's file; it can provide invaluable protection to an employer in the case of a future wrongful termination suit.

There are many conditions that constitute good cause for a rightful termination of an employee, such as:

- economic necessity (as cited by many corporations in recent years for huge employee scalebacks)
- breach of contract (when the employee violates a written agreement with the employer)
- incompetence, poor performance, or neglect of duty
- misconduct

- disobedience and insubordination
- intoxication or intemperance
- disloyalty (such as sharing trade secrets or customer lists with competitors).

Once you decide to terminate an employee, paper the file with written documentation of all the good causes justifying the termination. Do this as soon as possible, so you won't have to rely on memory if you are sued, possibly years later. In addition if possible, gather affidavits or written statements by other employees and company personnel who are aware of the employee's wrongdoing. Bolstering the file with these statements will increase your ability to defend against a wrongful termination suit.

In-House Training

Your vulnerability to lawsuits may be reduced dramatically if you conduct periodic employee training meetings. In such meetings, the employers discuss the scope of employment of the employees, including their duties and responsibility and what limitations are placed on them. Negligence in properly instructing employees in the proper performance of work and proper supervision makes an employer liable for injuries to employees, particularly when they use dangerous equipment or vehicles.

Proper supervision is critical. In one case, the employer was held liable for the racial harassment by employees of a coworker because the employer failed to take reasonable steps to prevent the barrage of threats and racial attacks against the employee.[12]

The Written Employment Contract

A well-drafted employment agreement can be of immeasurable value to an employer. The contract should set forth the duties, responsibilities, obligations, and restrictions of an employee. Such a contract can aid you if you are sued by an employee for wrongful termination by showing that the employee was not performing the duties as required by the contract. An employment agreement can also help you in a suit for negligent acts of an employee if the contract establishes that the employee was acting outside the scope of his or her employment when the negligent act occurred.

Another tool that can help protect your assets is an employee handbook that clearly delineates the duties and responsibilities of each employee. The handbook should enumerate in detail those acts that are expressly prohibited by employees. The employer should conduct periodic interviews with each employee where the employee's duties and responsibilities and performance are discussed, and make notations in the employee's file about the content of the interview. In addition to these individual employee interviews, there should also be staff meetings for further education and explanation of duties and responsibilities.

By following these guidelines, you can substantially reduce your vulnerability to lawsuits caused or initiated by your employees.

Action Checklist

❑ Draft an employment contract for each employee, spelling out the duties, responsibilities, obligations, and restrictions of each employee.

❑ Regular ongoing employee training meetings are a must. They should be held at least annually.

❑ Create an employee handbook that delineates the duties and responsibilities of each employee.

❑ Conduct regular interviews with employees to discuss their duties, responsibilities, and performance.

❑ Consult an expert in labor law regarding additional steps you should take to educate employees on topics of current concern such as sexual harassment.

Chapter 25

How to Sell Your Business Without Future Liability

A retired seventy-seven-year-old man and his seventy-six-year-old wife came to me for help. They were in a financial nightmare, and there was little I could do. Six years earlier they had sold their small retail clothing business to a trusted longtime employee. They had asked for nothing down, requiring monthly payments from the buyer for the next twenty years. The agreement the couple had with the buyer was no more than some paperwork scratched out on one side of a sheet of paper.

The buyer had good intentions but didn't have the skills required to operate a retail business. When customers found out that the prior owners were no longer running the business, they began shopping elsewhere, and within two years the business was closed. The inventory was gone and liens were placed against the business real estate. The monthly payments were to have constituted the majority of the retirement income for the retiring owners, and they had received little of that income during the past two years.

Here are the mistakes the sellers made that led to this catastrophe:

- They sold the business without an effectively drawn written agreement. The attorney fees they saved turned out to cost them a great deal.
- They did not require a substantial down payment from the new owner.
- They conveyed title to the real estate to the buyer. He then mortgaged the property, and now the sellers have to repay that obligation also.
- Even though the buyer was a trusted employee, they should have required a credit check, and possibly additional cosigners or guarantors, so they would have recourse against others in the event of default by the buyer.
- The sellers should have maintained a secured interest in all of the equipment and fixtures so that they would have preferential rights to those assets in the event of a business liquidation.
- The sellers should have required monthly accountings of the inventory sold.
- The sales agreement should have been two agreements, not one. The first agreement should have related specifically to the real estate so that in event of default, foreclosure proceedings could have been initiated immediately. The second sales agreement should have been for the equipment, inventory, and goodwill. In law, different remedies are available for real estate and personal property.

Don't make mistakes like this when you sell your business. Consult an experienced attorney who is familiar with the multiple issues that are involved in this kind of transaction. The potential for disaster is just too great for you to consider completing this kind of transaction yourself.

Future Lawsuits Against the Sold Business

When you sell your business, you must always anticipate that the business you have just sold will likely be involved in a lawsuit sometime in the future. The lawsuit may be for an act or an event that occurred prior to the date of sale. If so, you, as seller, will probably be joined into the action as a defendant. The business may be sued for an event that occurred after the date of sale. If so, the new purchaser is responsible. However, if the sales agreement is not correctly structured and the seller's involvement not substantially restricted in the activities of the sold business, then the seller could be named in the lawsuit as well. This is often the case where the seller agrees to allow his name to be used in the sold business, or agrees to provide management, guidance, and advice or general supervision to the purchaser. In such cases, the seller may find himself caught in a web of lawsuits years after he sold the business, and could even be found fully liable for acts of the new purchaser.

To protect yourself as seller, consider restricting your liability through special clauses in the sales contract. In one sales agreement, the seller and the buyer agreed to the following: "Any claim of liability arising out of the business . . . occurring before [date] shall be borne 75% by seller and 25% by purchaser, provided such claim is asserted within three years of the date of this agreement. . . . In no event shall seller's liability ... exceed the aggregate sum of [amount]."[1]

The courts are much more inclined to uphold this kind of arrangement where it is agreed to in the sales agreement. Without the benefit of this kind of wording, the courts are fairly uniform in holding the seller liable for events that occurred while the seller owned the business.

The purchaser may demand that the seller indemnify him from lawsuits for preexisting actions. To indemnify the buyer, the seller agrees to assume all liability for such actions. For example, one contract provided that the "seller will indemnify and hold buyer harmless against ... all liabilities ... of any nature, whether absolute, accrued, contingent or otherwise, existing at [date]."[2]

This provision proved to be of immense value to the purchaser when the business was sued on a product liability claim for personal injuries sustained from an earlier accident.

There is no substitute for specific provisions in the sales agreement. Obviously, the purchaser will want the provisions of the sales contract to be in his favor, and the seller will want provisions that are in his favor. Often, the party who drafts the agreement prevails in actions, since his attorney will take particular care to draft the agreement in favor of his client. Be careful though: Anything ambiguous in the contract will generally be interpreted against the drafter.

Here are some examples of how various clauses might be used. In one case a seller warranted in the sales agreement that the financial and tax disclosures were accurate. When the buyer discovered an accounting error that resulted in a substantial additional tax liability, the court held the sellers responsible because they had violated the written warranty contained in the sales agreement.[3]

In a similar case, a seller warranted that the inventory was salable for at least $1 million. When the purchasers sold the inventory and received substantially less, they sued. The court awarded the buyers over $500,000 for breach of warranty by the seller.[4]

The warranty must be carefully worded to be effective. A buyer sued when equipment he had purchased broke down several months after purchase. The seller had warranted that the equipment was in good condition "at the date of sale," and the courts held that the warranty of good condition did not extend to future performance, so the seller was not liable.[5]

Environmental Concerns

Special care must be taken by the parties to a sales agreement if the business being sold involves toxic chemicals or other substances that can potentially contaminate the environment. The federal and state governments can hold responsible both seller and buyer—that is, anyone whose hands have touched title to the property can be held liable for fines and costs of cleanup. Under both federal and state laws the "responsible party doctrine" is far-reaching and very inclusionary of multiple parties. In one case, the buyer of a paint business was sued for improper disposal of hazardous wastes. The seller of the business was also held liable for the cleanup costs as a responsible party. Unfortunately, the seller had not anticipated this potential problem, and the sales agreement made no provision for the buyer to indemnify the seller.[6]

In another case, the sales agreement included a clause that transferred all environmental liabilities to the purchaser. The land turned out to be contaminated, and the court held that the purchaser alone was liable for the cleanup costs.[7] A word of caution: A different result could have occurred if the purchaser had been insolvent or out of business. Both the state and the federal governments, armed with environmental protection laws, may proceed against both the buyer and the seller, regardless of clauses in the sales agreement. But indemnification clauses will give one party the right to collect from the other if forced to pay.

An Advanced Strategy

Because there are so many rules of law under which a seller may be named as a defendant in a lawsuit against the sold business, attorneys frequently have the seller transfer ownership of the business to a corporation or limited liability company before it is sold. To enhance lawsuit protection even more, many attorneys will incorporate a business under the laws of Delaware or Nevada because of the advanced lawsuit protection these states afford officers and directors of corporations. Because of this advanced lawsuit protection strategy, in the event of a suit, an EPA claim, or other legal action, the purchaser generally will have to pursue the protected corporation from which he or she purchased the property, rather than the unprotected individual. This technique is used infrequently, but it has been effective in protecting sellers of businesses. Be sure to discuss it with your attorney if you are planning to sell your business.

Action Checklist

Pay attention to the following factors when you decide to sell your business:

❑ Always put your agreement in writing.

❑ Always have your own attorney write the contract. Often the party that prevails in a subsequent suit is the party whose attorney has drafted the agreement.

❑ Enter into two separate agreements: one for real estate and the other for personal property, inventory, and so on.

❑ Discuss with your attorney the advisability of setting up a new entity to become the seller of the business.

❑ Always check the credit-worthiness of the buyer and secure additional collateralization or guarantors or co-makers for the agreement.

❑ Request a sizable down payment, and maintain security interest in the inventory and equipment so that in a default by the buyer your legal claim will be superior to the buyer's other creditors.

❑ Include specific warranties, depending on whether you are the buyer or the seller.

❑ Include a provision indemnifying you against any subsequent lawsuits pertaining to the sold business.

Chapter 26

A Review: Applying Asset Protection Principles

A very wealthy Idaho rancher with three grown children came to our office for help. He operated his ranch with his son, and he wanted me to structure their business and real estate holdings for maximum family protection.

The diagram on page 213 lists the entities I structured to hold the assets of the parents and son. (The two daughters did not own substantial assets, and so I did not have to re-structure their holdings.)

Now, can you answer the following questions?

1. Why was the ranching and farming operation structured as a C corporation?
2. Why was the corporation set up in Nevada when the ranch is located in Idaho?

I. Business Level Planning

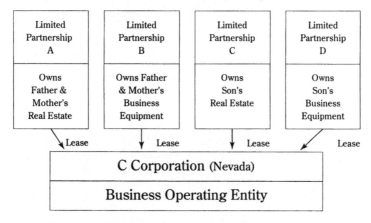

Limited Partnership A	Limited Partnership B	Limited Partnership C	Limited Partnership D
Owns Father & Mother's Real Estate	Owns Father & Mother's Business Equipment	Owns Son's Real Estate	Owns Son's Business Equipment

↓ Lease   ↓ Lease   ↓ Lease   ↓ Lease

C Corporation (Nevada)

Business Operating Entity

II. Personal Level Planning

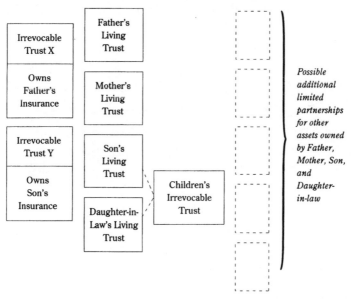

Irrevocable Trust X	Father's Living Trust
Owns Father's Insurance	Mother's Living Trust
Irrevocable Trust Y	Son's Living Trust
Owns Son's Insurance	Daughter-in-Law's Living Trust

Children's Irrevocable Trust

Possible additional limited partnerships for other assets owned by Father, Mother, Son, and Daughter-in-law

3. Why was the son listed as the only incorporator, the president, the secretary, and the treasurer?
4. Why was the stock owned 50 percent by the father and 50 percent by the son, and none owned by their respective spouses and children?
5. Why was half of the land conveyed to limited partnership A and the other half to limited partnership B?
6. Why were the respective wives not involved as officers and directors in the operating corporation?
7. Why was neither land nor equipment transferred to the corporation?
8. Why was 50 percent of the farming and ranching equipment transferred into limited partnership B and the remaining 50 percent into limited partnership D?
9. Why were two irrevocable trusts set up?
10. Why were four revocable trusts established?
11. Some advisers say that perfect asset protection is having the vulnerable client own nothing. Why do the individuals in this example own assets?
12. Why was a children's irrevocable trust set up for the son, but not for his mother or father?

If you can answer all these questions, it means that you have carefully studied the chapters of this book. Congratulations, you are now an expert in asset protection.

The Answers

The Plan for a Large and Complex Estate

1. Why was the ranching and farming operation structured as a C corporation?

A. Although both S corporations and C corporations afford asset protection, in this case the C corporation offered some income tax advantages that the S corporation did not. For example, the C corporation can have a medical reimbursement plan, while the S corporation cannot. That means that the C corporation can pay and deduct the family's medical bills, rather than the bills being paid personally and being subject to a deduction floor of 7.5 percent of income on a personal tax return. The C corporation can also deduct the cost of life insurance it provides to employees, which cannot be done by an S corporation. See Chapter 17 for a discussion of S corporations and C corporations.

2. Why was the corporation set up in Nevada when the ranch is located in Idaho?

A. The farming corporation was structured in the state of Nevada even though operations were in Idaho because in the event of a lawsuit, the rules governing the liability of officers and directors are generally governed by the laws of the state of incorporation. See Chapter 20 for a more detailed discussion.

3. Why was the son listed as the only incorporator, the president, the secretary, and the treasurer?

A. Why put several necks in the legal noose when one will do? I picked the son, who agreed to assume any liability as incorporator and officer, rather than compounding risks by adding other family members to the roster of officers. This information was discussed in Chapter 18.

4. Why was the stock owned 50 percent by the father and 50 percent by the son, and none owned by their respective spouses and children?

A. I chose not to make them shareholders because the corporation was of limited value, since we kept most assets outside the corporation for asset protection. If a client has an already established corporation of sizable value, I will not include the wife and children as officers or directors, but I will include them as shareholders. For example, in a dangerous corporation, the father might be the only director and officer, but he would generally own only 1 percent of the stock. The rest of the stock could be owned by his wife and children or, in a more advanced situation, I would put all of the stock into a family limited partnership. You will find more about this subject in Chapter 19.

5. Why was half of the land conveyed to limited partnership A and the other half to limited partnership B?

A. All of the father's real estate was transferred into family limited partnership A with the father as a general partner and the two daughters also having substantial ownership interests. The daughters, though not involved in the ranching operation, received a substantial interest in the partnership so that revenues from the ranching operation, in the form of rents, could provide revenue to them. In this way, the father and mother could pass the farming operation to the son and yet still have the daughters receive some income benefits from the large estate.

Limited partnership B was set up to own the potentially dangerous equipment. It is often wise to separate ownership of equipment from the entity that owns the real estate. The father was the sole general partner, and the wife and children were limited partners, so they were protected if a suit occurred because of an accident involving the dangerous equipment. Chapter 19 explains more about creating separate entities.

6. Why were the respective wives not involved as officers and directors in the operating corporation?

A. I did not want the wife or children to be officers or directors in the corporation because in lawsuits brought against a corporation, the officers and directors of the corporation are often named as defendants. Although they were not shareholders, they could have been with a sizable degree of security. See Chapter 18 for more discussion of this complex concept.

I am often asked to involve the children in the corporation, and I am happy to do so. They can be shareholders or they can be employees, but if I am the attorney, they will not be officers or directors. Why increase the size of the group to which a potential creditor can look for recovery?

7. Why was neither land nor equipment transferred to the corporation?

A. The assets were not transferred into the corporation because in the event of a lawsuit, wrongful termination action, or negligence involving injury or death, a judgment against the corporation could result in the loss of all corporate assets. See Chapter 18 for a more detailed discussion of this subject.

8. Why was 50 percent of the farming and ranching equipment transferred into limited partnership B and the remaining 50 percent into limited partnership D?

A. Father and son had farmed together for many years and owned over $2 million of equipment. Half of those assets were put into a separate partnership so that the son could share the lease income with his children. The other half was placed in a separate limited partnership so that the father could share the lease income with his daughters, providing some assistance to them.

The four limited partnerships set up in this huge operation would enter into written lease agreements with the ranching corporation.

9. Why were two irrevocable trusts set up?

A. Irrevocable trust X holds all the life insurance belonging to the father. Because the trust is irrevocable, at the death of the father, his life insurance will not be taxed in his estate. It goes estate-tax free to his spouse, and equally importantly, it goes estate-tax free to his children. In this case, because the son was already financially secure, the two daughters were named as the beneficiaries of the irrevocable trust so that they would one day receive cash from the insurance estate.

Similarly, irrevocable trust Y was established to hold the life insurance on the son. His wife was named as beneficiary of that trust, with his four children as successor beneficiaries. In this way, all the insurance on his life will ultimately be divided equally among his children. Chapter 10 explains this concept.

10. Why were four revocable trusts established?

A. A living trust was set up for the mother, father, son, and daughter-in-law. These trusts would hold all assets, including partnership interests owned by the four parties. In this way, they will avoid probate at the death of any of these family members. In addition, each living trust included a marital trust (an "A" trust) so there would be no estate taxes if either father or son were to die. Their respective estates would go to their spouses, free of any estate taxes and without probate.

11. Some advisers say that perfect asset protection is having the vulnerable client own nothing. Why do the individuals in this example own assets?

A. I never allow my clients to be completely without assets. I always leave some assets exposed, there for a potential creditor to seize if an award is rendered against my client. In this way the creditor receives something for his efforts, and that might preclude the judge applying the Fraudulent Conveyances Act.

12. Why was a children's irrevocable trust set up for the son, but not for his mother or father?

A. Because the son's four children are all minors, we established a separate children's trust, known as a 2503(c) children's trust. This entity holds the limited partnership interests of the minor children, which provides greater estate planning protection for their interests in the limited partnership. Many tax attorneys believe that the interests of minor children should be held by irrevocable children's trusts to provide added legal protection and to avoid any imputation by the Internal Revenue Service that could make the partnership interest taxable as part of the estate of the mother and father.

All of this may sound a little complex, and for good reason—it is. Effective asset protection is not simple, and frequently involves the use of many advanced legal tools, the understanding of which is usually beyond the training and expertise of general practitioners of estate planning.

Is all this complexity worth it? You bet. When these clients came to our law firm, they were all involved in a general partnership, which meant that if anything went wrong and a massive lawsuit occurred, they could have lost everything—all the land, all the real estate, all the equipment, and even their homes. Every asset they owned was exposed because of the amateurism of their planning. They had been to the typical seminars on living trusts, but the trusts they had set up were only partially funded and would not have provided lawsuit protection. This meant that their estates would still have been subject to probate. Like millions of Americans, they had insufficiently planned their business entities and estates for today's complex world. The field of asset protection is beyond the scope of most estate planners. That is why many lawyers and estate planners come to our law firm for their own individual planning. Lawyers in your own city probably do the same, consulting with attorneys they know who are expert in these areas.

Chapter 27

How to Select an Asset Protection Attorney

Now that you have read this book, it is time to create your own total asset protection plan. The first step is to list the personal and business assets you need to protect. On the following page is a simple net worth worksheet that you can use to compile your assets and the debts against them.

Once you have completed your list of assets and debts, you need to find an attorney to help you restructure the ownership of your personal and business assets for maximum protection.

How to Select an Asset Protection Attorney

An asset protection attorney must have a firm grounding in tax law and estate planning. Here are some ways you can find an attorney to help you.

    1. Call your local bar association and request the names of

Assets	Fair Market Value	Debt	Net Worth	How Titled
I. Personal Assets				
1. Home				
2. Stocks/Equities				
3. Vehicles				
4. Risky assets (boats, planes, and so forth)				
5.				
6.				
7.				
Total Personal Assets Net Worth			$_____	

Assets	Fair Market Value	Debt	Net Worth	How Titled
II. Business Assets				
1. Real Estate				
2. Equipment				
3. Risky assets (dangerous equipment, airplanes and the like)				
4.				
5.				
6.				
7.				
8.				
Total Business Assets Net Worth				$ ___
Total Personal and Business Net Worth				$ ___

attorneys who are expert in asset protection or advanced estate planning.

2. Ask an attorney in general practice or your accountant to recommend an attorney knowledgeable in asset protection. Attorneys and accountants who are not expert in this particular field will nonetheless have attended professional meetings at which asset protection experts speak.

3. Talk to a friend or business associate who has created an asset protection plan for the name of the attorney who designed the plan for him or her.

4. If you cannot find an attorney through any of these methods, look in the Yellow Pages. Briefly interview the attorneys you choose over the phone to get an idea of their qualifications.

When you interview an attorney on the telephone, ascertain how many funded living trusts, limited partnerships, and limited liability companies he or she has set up during the past year. An attorney experienced in asset protection will be quite active in these areas. Ask the attorney to describe a recent client's situation, without divulging the client's name or confidential information, and the asset protection designed for that client. Don't be afraid to ask hard questions. You have spent your lifetime accumulating your assets and you deserve to find someone who is knowledgeable and experienced to help you protect them.

After you have interviewed several attorneys by telephone, you will probably have found one who sounds knowledgeable and with whom you feel you'll be able to establish some rapport. Arrange to meet with the attorney to discuss how legal ownership for your property should be changed. When you visit the attorney, take a copy of this book with you. Review

Chapter 26 and the case studies in the appendix with the attorney and discuss the issues. You will quickly see whether the attorney understands the issues involved. If the attorney grasps the concepts well, you should take comfort that you are probably talking to an expert who can help you with your needs.

Here are some of the questions you and the attorney should discuss, and the answers you might expect. Here also are some possibly dangerous answers that reveal that the attorney is not familiar with the asset protection tools you have learned in this book and may not be able to adequately protect your assets.

Asset: Your Home

Question to Ask: In the event of a lawsuit, what form of ownership would provide superior asset protection?

Favorable Answers:

1. Limited partnership.
2. Limited liability company.
3. Holding title in the less vulnerable spouse's name or in her living trust.
4. An irrevocable trust.

Possibly Dangerous Answers:

1. It doesn't matter how you hold title; a creditor will take your home to the extent its equity exceeds the homestead exemption anyway.
2. Just keep everything in joint ownership and don't worry about it.

Asset: Stocks, Bonds, and Mutual Funds

Question to Ask: In the event of a lawsuit, what form of ownership would provide superior asset protection?

Favorable Answers:

1. Limited partnership.
2. Limited liability company.
3. Holding title in the less vulnerable spouse's name or in her living trust.
4. An irrevocable trust.

Possibly Dangerous Answers:

1. It doesn't matter how you hold title; a creditor will take your assets no matter what you do.
2. Just keep everything in joint ownership and don't worry about it.

Asset: Business Real Estate

Questions to Ask: 1. Should I keep business real estate in the same corporation in which I operate my business? 2. Should I separate my business real estate from my personal assets?

Favorable Answers:

1. It is frequently advisable to keep business real estate outside the business corporation to reduce its vulnerability to lawsuits, liens, and levies against the business operations.
2. Rather than owning the business real estate personally, it might be desirable to place business real estate in a limited partnership, limited liability company, or a children's trust and then lease it back to the business.

Possibly Dangerous Answers:

1. It's really not important to separate business real estate from your business operations or personal assets.
2. Just keep all the assets of your business together in your single business corporation. You don't want any complex ownership scheme complicating your life.

Asset: Business Equipment

Question to Ask: How should my business equipment be owned?

Favorable Answers:

1. It could be owned by the corporation.
2. It could be owned by a family trust, children's trust, limited liability company, or limited partnership and leased to the business corporation.

Possibly Dangerous Answer:
Don't worry about the remote possibility of a lawsuit. Just keep the business equipment in your own name, or in joint ownership with your spouse.

Other Asset Protection Issues

Question to Ask: In which state is it best to incorporate a business in?

Favorable Answers:

1. Nevada.
2. Delaware.

Possibly Dangerous Answer:
It really doesn't matter; all states are the same.

Question to Ask: How many limited partnerships or limited liability companies have you set up in the past three years?

Favorable Answer:
Five or more.

Possibly Dangerous Answers:

1. I've never personally set these up.
2. I've read about them and they are so complex that the IRS considers them illegal.
3. You will be audited frequently by the IRS if you use such entities.

Question to Ask: Would a children's or grandchildren's trust be beneficial to me?

Favorable Answers:

1. You can gain substantial asset protection with such entities.
2. You can save income taxes with these entities if the children or grandchildren are fourteen or older.

Possibly Dangerous Answer:
I don't recommend children's trusts because they are under constant assault by the IRS, and besides, they don't work anyway.

Question to Ask: Should I use one corporation or two to operate my business?

Favorable Answer:

If your business can be divided into two or more subparts, it may be advisable to use two separate corporations; in that way the assets of one corporation are insulated if the other corporation is sued.

Possibly Dangerous Answer:

Multiple corporations are far too complex. The simpler your business operations and asset ownership, the better off you will be.

Question to Ask: Explain to me how the charging order protects assets.

Favorable Answer:

The charging order generally restricts the creditor from seizing assets inside limited partnerships and limited liability companies. It is one of the most unique asset protection provisions there is.

Possibly Dangerous Answer:

I've never heard of a charging order before. All you really need to protect your assets is a living trust. (This question pointedly reveals the level of sophistication of the attorney. To date I have never met a general practitioner attorney who can answer this question.)

Of course, there are many more questions that you can ask your estate planner. However, these questions are sufficient to get some indication of how comfortable your adviser is with advanced asset protection strategies. If the adviser hedges or bluffs on most of the answers, or simply doesn't know the answers, it may be an indication that your estate planner is not very familiar with these rather complex inter-woven issues.

Each day, more and more attorneys are jumping on the asset protection bandwagon. It is important to choose an attorney thoroughly versed in the nuances of the law, since the field is very complex. If documents are improperly drawn, fatal flaws will allow easy unwinding of your protection plan and will enable creditors to seize your assets.

Over the years, I have seen much potential malpractice in this field and much amateurism. You cannot afford that—if the advanced estate planning and asset protection is done incorrectly, you could lose everything. Unfortunately, if your planning is incorrectly done and you suffer loss as a result, you may not be able to recover in a malpractice action against your attorney. This is because, in most situations, an attorney is generally not held to the standard of an expert estate planner. The legal standard for determining malpractice is generally: What would an average attorney in the local area have done for a client in similar circumstances? Unless most of the lawyers in your community are experts, a higher standard of expertise will not normally be applied. So don't assume that if something goes wrong, you will just sue the attorney for malpractice. Rather, carefully interview three or four estate planners and then pick one to help you devise the best system for protection of your hard-earned estate.

Appendix: A Case Study, with Variations

Protecting the Professional or Business Owner

Dr. Morrison was an obstetrician who was immensely concerned about his malpractice exposure. He had incorporated his medical practice, but he still felt vulnerable. He and his wife had built a moderate estate, which he wanted to protect. He had three children, a twenty-one-year-old son who was a premed junior at an Ivy League college, a nineteen-year-old daughter who was a freshman majoring in music at a private college, and a fifteen-year-old son who was a sophomore at a private high school.

Here are the asset protection steps I recommended for Dr. Morrison and his family.

Remove Your Wife as an Officer of the Medical Corporation. When a corporation is sued, sometimes the courts will "pierce the corporate veil," penetrating the corporate liability veil and holding the officers and directors of the corporation liable for damages. I prefer that only one neck be personally in the corporate liability noose.

Review Your Corporate Records and Tie up All Loose Ends. When you organize as a corporation, it is important that you operate as a corporation in every respect. Dr. Morrison was a busy professional who had never taken the time to issue corporate stock or record the minutes of the board of director meetings or the annual stockholder meetings. As a matter of fact, he hadn't even signed the minutes of the first organizational meeting held by the corporation.

These things may seem like trivial niceties, but in fact they could be the downfall of Dr. Morrison's entire estate. In order to gain a substantial degree of liability protection from incorporating, it is important that you look and act like a corporation at all times. About 80 percent of all corporations fail to comply with the basic requirements to gain liability protection, and they are at great risk of liability penetration, allowing full liability to fall squarely on the shoulders of the officers and directors.

Create a Fully Funded Living Trust for Both You and Your Wife. Because of Dr. Morrison's liability exposure, we put several of the properties that he and his wife owned in the wife's living trust, including their home. Because Dr. Morrison was reluctant to give up control over these assets, we made him a cotrustee with his wife over the wife's trust, so he could have access to the assets, yet ownership was retained by his wife. Her assets will generally not be vulnerable to her husband's creditors, and vice versa. We could have simply conveyed the assets directly to Mrs. Morrison, not using a trust at all, but the living trust has the added advantage of avoiding probate costs. In addition, the funded trust provides added protection against the possibility that the courts could hold the wife as "constructive trustee" for her husband, thus allowing the husband's creditors to reach the assets.

Create an Irrevocable Insurance Trust. If Dr. Morrison is sued, the cash values in his insurance policies won't be reachable by his creditors if the policies are owned by an irrevocable insurance trust. We named Dr. Morrison's children as beneficiaries of the irrevocable insurance trust, so that the proceeds of the policies can pass estate-tax-free to them when he dies. If we had not set up the insurance trust, the cash value of the policies would be vulnerable. In addition, although assets can pass free of estate tax to a spouse, the insurance proceeds for all policies owned by Dr. Morrison would have been fully taxed upon his death if the beneficiary were anyone other than his wife.

Create a Children's Trust. A children's trust offers both asset protection benefits and income tax savings. Dr. Morrison's creditors cannot reach the assets of the trust, and the trust can reduce taxes as trust income is taxed to the children at their lower tax brackets rather than to Dr. and Mrs. Morrison on their joint income tax return. Dr. Morrison funded the children's trust with cash, and the trust then used the money to purchase a new car and some equipment, which it leased to the medical corporation. The lease payments are deducted by the corporation, taxed at the children's tax rates, and accumulated to pay tuition for the children. Once the children reach majority, the trustee can terminate the children's trust, and the accumulated assets can be contributed to a family limited partnership controlled by Dr. Morrison as general partner. The children's trust is therefore an ideal means of building wealth with significant income-tax deductions and later allowing full control of that wealth through the termination of the children's trust and the transfer of those assets to the family limited partnership.

Establish a Business Trust to Hold Title to the Apartment Building. The apartment building is a dangerous asset with great vulnerability to lawsuits, so it must be isolated from the rest of Dr. Morrison's estate. Under the business trust, Dr. Morrison is trustee, so he has full control over the apartment building and any assets he places in the trust in the future. Mrs. Morrison is the beneficiary of the trust, so she has all the benefits of ownership without the liability exposure. If Dr. Morrison is sued, the assets held by the business trust are protected. The apartment building provides some tax shelter, and those tax-shelter benefits can generally flow through to Dr. Morrison and his wife on their joint income tax return.

Establish Family Limited Partnership #1 to Hold Investment Assets. Dr. Morrison and his wife are general partners, owning 5 percent of this partnership, and the children are limited partners with a 95 percent interest. As general partners, Dr. and Mrs. Morrison have complete control over the assets, even though they own only a 5 percent interest. The family limited partnership is very effective for asset protection, because if Dr. Morrison is sued, the most that his creditors can receive is a charging order, meaning they can receive 5 percent of the income of the partnership, but none of the assets. Even if one of the children is sued, the partnership assets will not be reachable by a judgment creditor. In addition, because 95 percent of the partnership is owned by the children, the assets are growing outside Dr. Morrison's estate, so when he dies that asset growth will pass estate-tax-free to his children. And when assets are sold, most of the income will be spread among the children, which is an income tax advantage if they are in a lower income tax bracket than their parents.

Set up Family Limited Partnership #2 to Hold Rental Properties. Dr. Morrison and his wife have four single-family rentals, which we transferred to this limited partnership. Dr. Morrison is the general partner, but he owns just 1 percent of this partnership, and his wife owns the rest as limited partner. Dr. Morrison has full control over the properties, and the depreciation and other tax benefits still flow through to him and his wife on their joint income tax return. Forming a second limited partnership to hold these rental properties has two advantages. First of all, had we placed these properties into Family Limited Partnership #1, most of the tax benefits would have flowed to the children, because they own most of that limited partnership. Secondly, we plan for the worst: If one of the partnerships is involved in a lawsuit some day, it could result in the loss of all of the assets owned by that partnership. By creating more than one partnership, we have multiplied Dr. Morrison's asset protection benefits.

Variation #1. Dr. Morrison's Wife Is a Neurosurgeon

I cannot think of a situation in which a client faces more lawsuit vulnerability and potential for loss than the case where both spouses are high-risk physicians. In this situation, the best approach is to multiply the asset protection benefits of the family limited partnership by creating a partnership for each vulnerable asset. Instead of conveying the apartment building into a business trust, and conveying all four rental properties to one family limited partnership, we would create a partnership for each property. Instead of Mrs. Morrison owning 99 percent of the limited partnership interests, she and her husband would each own 40 percent partnership interests, with the children as limited partners owning 20 percent. With both spouses vulnerable to lawsuit, multiple family limited partnerships offer the most asset protection. The doctors' creditors cannot get any assets of the limited partnerships. They would be granted a charging order, but that charging order gives them no vote or management control, so they can't remove the doctors as general partners. They are entitled to receive any income distributed by the partnerships, but they can't force the partnerships to distribute income to them. Because the creditor is designated to receive the income when distributed, the creditor will have to pay income taxes on the partnership income as it is earned, even though it isn't distributed to him. Rather than suffering the consequence of paying tax on income not received, the creditor will likely forego the charging order altogether, leaving the income and assets of the limited partnerships untouched.

Variation #2. Dr. Morrison Is Unmarried

For unmarried clients, in lieu of general partnerships or business trusts, I often recommend multiple entities, using C corporations for businesses and limited partnerships for real estate that has tax benefits that I want to pass through to my client. If my client has children or other family members for whom he wants to provide, I will use one or more family limited partnerships with other family members owning the majority of the interests as limited partners, and my client, the single person, controlling the partnership through his small general partnership interest.

Notes

2. Avoiding Liability for the Acts of Your Children

1. *Labadie v Semler*, 585 N.E. 2d 862 (Ohio Ct. App. 1990).
2. *Gardiner v Gallacher*, 553 N.Y.S. 2d 449 (N.Y. All. Div. 1990).
3. *Keely v Allstate Insurance Co.*, 835 P. 2d 584 (Colo. Ct. App. 1991).
4. *Roger v Voyles*, 797 S.W. 2d 844 (Mo. Ct. App. 1990).
5. In re *William George T.*, 599 A. 2d 886 (Md. Ct. Spec. App. 1992).
6. *Schwartz v Licht*, 570 N.Y.S. 2d 83 (N.Y. App. Div. 1991).
7. *Huston v Konieczny*, 556 N.E. 2d 505 (Ohio 1990).

3. The Dangers of Volunteer Work

1. *Infant C v Boy Scouts of America, Inc.*, 391 S.E. 2d 322 (Va. 1990).

4. The Risks of Serving as an Officer or Director

1. *K.C. Roofing Center v On Top Roofing, Inc.*, 807 S.W. 2d 545 (Mo. Ct. App. 1991).
2. *Wetzel v United States*, 802 F. Supp. 1451 (S.D. Miss. 1992).

5. Avoiding Liability for Giving Advice

1. *Kelly v Roussalis,* 776 P. 2d 1016 (Wy. 1989).
2. *Bienz v Central Suffolk Hospital,* 557 N.Y.S. 2d 139 (N.Y. App. Div. 1990).
3. *Parker v Carnahan,* 772 S.W. 2d 151 (Tex. Ct. App. 1989).
4. *Selden v Burnett,* 754 P. 2d 256 (Alaska 1988).
5. *Rosenblum, Inc., v Alder,* 461 A. 2d 138 (N.J. 1983).
6. *Cohen v Prudential-Bache Securities, Inc.,* 713 F. Supp. 653 (S.D. N.Y. 1989).
7. *Alton v Wyland,* 595 N.E. 2d 993 (Ohio Ct. App. 1991).
8. *Atkinson v Haug,* 622 A. 2d 983 (Pa. Super. Ct. 1993).
9. *Federal Insurance Co. v Mallardi,* 696 F. Supp. 875 (S.D.N.Y. 1988).
10. *Gilmore v Berg,* 761 F. Supp. 358 (D.N.J. 1991).

6. Avoiding the Pitfalls of Allowing Your Name to Be Used by Others

1. *Rottinghaus v Howell,* 666 P. 2d 899 (Wash. Ct. App. 1983).
2. *Hanberry v Hearst Corporation,* 81 Cal. Rptr. 519 (Cal. Ct. App. 1969).
3. *Frances T. v Village Green Owner's Ass'n,* 229 Cal. Rptr. 456 (1986).
4. *Moseley v Commercial State Bank,* 457 So. 2d 967 (Ala. 1984).
5. *Continental Waste System, Ind. v Zoso Partnership,* 727 F. Supp. 1143 (N.D. Ill. 1989).
6. *Hommel v Micco,* 602 N.E. 2d 1259 (Ohio Ct. App. 1991).

7. The Dangers of Guaranteeing Obligations

1. *Farmers State Bank, Grafton v Huebner,* 475 N.W. 2d 640 (Iowa Ct. App. 1991).
2. *E.B.M. v V.W.,* 586 So. 2d 230 (Ala. Civ. App. 1991).
3. *Palmer v Student Loan Finance Corp.,* 153 B.R. 888 (D.S.D. 1993).
4. *Federal Deposit Insurance Corp. v Neitzel,* 769 F. Supp. 346 (D. Kan. 1991).

10. How Living Trusts Can Protect Your Assets

1. In re *Cowles,* 143 B.R. 5,7 (D. Mass. 1992).
2. In re *Hersloff,* 147 B.R. 262 (M.D. Fla. 1992).
3. *Walgren v Dolan,* 276 Cal. Rptr. 554, 558 (Cal. Ct. App. 1990).

11. Protecting Your Home from Lawsuits

1. *United States v Nat'l Bank of Commerce,* 472 U.S. 713 (1985).
2. *Perry v Williamson,* 824 S.W. 2d 869 (Ky. 1992).
3. *Burrell v Meads,* 569 N.E. 2d 637 (Idaho 1991).
4. *Curtis v DeAtley,* 663 P. 2d 1089 (Ind. 1983).

12. Selling Property Without Being Sued

1. *Stewart v Isabell,* 399 N.W. 2d 440, 444 (Mich. Ct. App. 1987).
2. *Posner v Davis,* 395 N.E. 2d 133 (Ill. Ct. App. 1979).
3. *Andrews v Casagrande,* 804 P. 2d 800 (Ariz. Ct. App. 1991).
4. *Kissel v Rosenbaum,* 579 N.E. 2d 1322 (Ind. Ct. App. 1991).
5. *Laborde v DeBlanc,* 587 So. 2d 58 (La. Ct. App. 1991).
6. *O'Connor v Scott,* 533 So. 2d 241 (Ala. 1988).
7. *VanGessel v Folds,* 569 N.E. 2d 141 (Ill. Ct. App. 1991).
8. *C. Lambert & Assoc., Inc., v Horizon Corp.,* 748 P. 2d 504 (N.M. 1988).
9. *Wagner v Butler,* 757 P. 2d 779 (Mont. 1988).

13. Surviving Bankruptcy with Your Assets Intact

1. *United States v Delinger,* 982 F. 2d 233, 236–37 (7th Cir. 1992).
2. *Knapp v Applewhite,* 146 B. R. 294 (M.D. Fla. 1992).
3. *Hopkins Illinois Elevator Co. v Pentell,* 777 F. 2d 1281 (7th Cir. 1985).
4. *Murray v Mares,* 147 B.R. 688 (E.D. Va. 1992).

14. How to Protect Your Assets in Divorce

1. *Pajak v Pajak,* 385 S.E. 2d 384 (W. Va. 1989).

2. *Pontorno v Pontorno,* 569 N.Y.S. 2d 120 (N.Y. App. Div. 1991).

15. How to Protect Your Personal Assets When Your Business Is Sued

1. *Vuitch v Furr,* 482 A. 2d 811 (D.C. Ct. App. 1984).
2. In re *Crabtree,* 39 B.R. 718 (E.D. Tenn. 1984).
3. In re *Telemark Management Co., Inc.,* 43 B.R. 579 (W.D. Wis. 1984).
4. *United States v Diviner,* 822 F. 2d 960, 961 (10th Cir. 1987).
5. *Central Business Forms, Inc., v N-Sure Systems, Inc.,* 540 So. 2d 1029 (La. Ct. App. 1989). *

16. Choosing the Best Insurance for You

1. *Buttelworth v Westfield Insurance Co.,* 535 N.E. 2d 320 (Ohio Ct. App. 1987).
2. *Farmers Insurance Company of Arizona v Wiechnick,* 801 P. 2d 501 (Ariz. Ct. App. 1990).
3. *Oelhalfen v Towe Insurance Company,* 492 N.W. 2d 321 (Wis. Ct. App. 1992).

18. The Advantages of Corporations for Businesses and Professionals

1. *Polokoff v Palmer,* 593 N.Y.S. 2d 129 (N.Y. App. Div. 1993), and *Krouner v Koplovitz,* 572 N.Y.S. 2d 959, 962 (N.Y. App. Div. 1991).
2. *Gershung v Martin McFall Messenger Anesthesia Professional Assoc.,* 539 So. 2d 1131 (Fla. 1989).
3. *Boyd, Payne, Gates & Farthing v Payne, Gates, Farthing & Radd, P.C.,* 422 S.E. 2d 784 (Va. 1992).
4. *Gleicher v Schachner,* 563 N.Y.S. 2d 1010, 1011 (N.Y. Civ. Ct. 1990).

19. Limited Partnerships Will Protect Your Assets

1. *Martinez v Koelling,* 421 N.W. 2d 1, 3 (Neb. 1988).
2. *Catalina Mortgage Co., Inc. v Monier,* 800 P. 2d 574 (Ariz. 1990).

3. *Wayne Smith Construction Co., Inc., v Wolman, Duberstein & Thompson,* 604 N.E. 2d 157 (Ohio 1992).
4. *Fanelli v Adler,* 516 N.Y.D. 2d 716, 717 (N.Y. App. Div. 1987).
5. *Bank of Bethesda v Koch,* 408 A. 2d 767 (Md. Ct. Spec. App. 1979).
6. *United States Shoe Corp. v Beard,* 463 F. Supp. 754 (S.D. Ala. 1979).

21. Avoiding the Dangers of Handshake Agreements

1. *Learning Works, Inc., v The Learning Annex, Inc.,* 830 F. 2d 541 (4th Cir. 1987).
2. *Bayside Health Club, Inc., v Weidel,* 565 N.Y.S. 2d 560 (N.Y. App. Div. 1991).

22. How Business Assets Should Be Held

1. *Ross v Manhattan Chelsea Assoc.,* 598 N.Y.S. 2d 502 (N.Y. App. Div. 1993).
2. *Rivete v LeBlanc,* 600 So. 2d 1358 (La. Ct. App. 1992).
3. *Hideca Petroleum Corp. v Tampimex Oil International, Ltd.,* 740 S.W. 2d 838, 843 (Tex. Ct. App. 1987).
4. *Hornsby v Hornsby's Stores, Inc.,* 734 F. Supp. 302, 308 (N.D. Ill. 1990).
5. In re *Phillips Petroleum Securities Litigation,* 738 F. Supp. 825, 838 (D. Del. 1990).
6. *Wm. Passalacqua Builders, Inc., v Resnick Developers South, Inc.,* 933 F. 2d 131 (2nd Cir. 1991).
7. *Craig v Lake Asbestos of Quebec,* 843 F. 2d 145, 152 (3rd Cir. 1988).
8. *Dannasch v Bifulco,* 585 N.Y.S. 2d 360 (N.Y. App. Div. 1992).
9. *Ed Moore Advertising Agency, Inc., v Shapiro,* 508 N.Y.S. 2d (N.Y. App. Div. 1986).
10. *Dufresene v Regency Realty, Inc., of Hilton Head Island,* 366 So. 2d 256 (S.C. 1987).

11. *Airflow Houston, Inc., v Theriot,* 849 S.W. 2d 928 (Tex. Ct. App. 1993).

23. How to Protect Against Customer Lawsuits

1. *Medical Mutual Liability Ins. Society of Maryland v Evans,* 604 A. 2d 934 (Md. Ct. Spec. App. 1992).
2. *Royal v Colorado State Personnel Board,* 722 P. 2d 1020 (Colo. Ct. App. 1986).
3. *Jones v Grewe,* 234 Cal. Rptr. 717 (Cal. Ct. App. 1987).

24. How to Protect Against Lawsuits Involving Employees

1. *Love v Liberty Mutual Ins. Co.,* 760 P. 2d 1085 (Ariz. Ct. App. 1988).
2. *Clover v Snowbird Ski Resort,* 808 P. 2d 1037 (Utah 1991).
3. *Bauer v Markovich,* 484 N.W. 2d 437 (Minn. Ct. App. 1992).
4. *Schneider v Buckman,* 433 N.W. 2d 98 (Minn. 1988).
5. *Robinson v KFC National Management Co.,* 525 N.E. 2d 1028 (Ill. Ct. App. 1988).
6. *Callahan v Boston Edison Co.,* 509 N.E. 2d 1208 (Mass. Ct. App. 1987).
7. *Texas Dept. of Human Services v Green,* 855 S.W. 2d 136 (Tex. Ct. App. 1993).
8. *Sanchez v Life Care Center of America, Inc.,* 855 P. 2d 1256 (Wy. 1993).
9. *Siekawitch v Washington Beek Producers, Inc.,* 793 P. 2d 994 (Wash. Ct. App. 1990).
10. *Coit Drapery Cleaners, Inc., v Sequoia Insurance Co.,* 18 Cal. Rptr. 2d 692 (Cal. Ct. App. 1993).
11. *Chicago Board of Options Exchange, Inc., v Harbor Insurance Co.,* 738 F. Supp. 1184 (N.D. Ill. 1990).
12. *Hunter v Allis-Chalmers Corp., Engine Division,* 797 F. 2d 1417 (7th Cir. 1986).

25. How to Sell Your Business Without Future Liability

1. *Seattle Northwest Securities Corp. v SDG Holding Co., Inc.,* 812 P. 2d 488, 491 (Wash. Ct. App. 1991).

2. *American Standard, Inc., v Goodman Equipment Co.*, 578 So. 2d 1083, 1084 (Ala. 1991).
3. *Blodgett Supply Co., Inc., v U.P.F. Jorgs and Co.*, 617 A. 2d 123 (Vt. 1992).
4. *Shepherd v Aaron Rents, Inc.*, 430 S.E. 2d 67 (Ga. Ct. App. 1993).
5. *Sperry v Papastamos*, 601 N.Y.S. 2d 720 (N.Y. App. Div. 1993).
6. *Allied Corp. v Acme Solvents Reclaiming*, 812 F. Supp. 125 (N.D. Ill. 1993).
7. *John S. Boyd Co., Inc., v Boston Gas Co.*, 992 F. 2d 401 (1st Cir. 1993).

Index